Reflecting Antiquity

Modern Glass Inspired by Ancient Rome

David Whitehouse

WITH CONTRIBUTIONS BY

William Gudenrath

Mark Taylor and David Hill

Karol Wight

Dunja Zobel-Klein and Michael J. Klein

The Corning Museum of Glass, Corning, New York

Editor
Richard W. Price

Design and Typography
Jacolyn S. Saunders

Photographic Supervisor
Nicholas L. Williams

Researcher and Proofreader
Mary B. Chervenak

Rights and Reproductions
Jill Thomas-Clark

Reference Librarian
Gail P. Bardhan

Standard Book Number: 978-0-87290-167-4
Library of Congress Control Number: 2007926944

Cover Images

Background: *Ribbon glass cup. Roman Empire, about 25 B.C.–A.D. 50. D. 8.6 cm. The Corning Museum of Glass (72.1.11).*

Foreground: *Ribbon glass bowl. Italy, Venice, Compagnia di Venezia e Murano (C.V.M.), Vincenzo Moretti (1835–1901), about 1880. H. 6.2 cm, D. (rim) 11.2 cm. The Corning Museum of Glass (50.3.76).*

Contents

Directors' Foreword

Michael Brand
Director, The J. Paul Getty Museum

David Whitehouse
Executive Director, The Corning Museum of Glass

GLASS IS A MEDIUM that is familiar to us all. We drink from glass vessels, glass windows allow the sun to illuminate our homes, and food is safely stored in glass containers. Glass played just as important a role in the lives of the ancients, and in many of the same ways. Visitors to our museums are frequently unaware that glass has been manufactured for thousands of years, and they marvel at the objects that were made as early as the second millennium B.C. They are also unaware that many of the techniques used to fashion glass into beautifully decorated shapes have been in existence since at least the first century B.C. These ancient techniques, and their impact on glassmakers in the modern period, provide the impetus for "Reflecting Antiquity: Modern Glass Inspired by Ancient Rome."

This exhibition examines the role that archeology played in vitalizing the modern glass industry. As archeological exploration began in Italy and elsewhere around the Mediterranean in the 18th and 19th centuries, fragmentary and whole glass vessels were uncovered along with many other material remains. Modern glassmakers were astounded at the rich variety of glass vessels that had been manufactured in antiquity, using techniques that were unfamiliar to them. They set about replicating these ancient techniques, first by trying to reproduce Roman masterpieces such as the Portland Vase, and then by interpreting them anew with their own designs and shapes. The results of this experimentation led to the formation of such commercial endeavors as the English cameo glass industry, the Rheinische Glashütten A.G. in Ehrenfeld, and the Compagnia di Venezia e Murano (C.V.M.) in Venice. This rediscovery continues today as glassmakers and scientists study the techniques and materials used by ancient glassmakers.

The exhibition is the product of a collaboration between Dr. Karol Wight, curator of antiquities at The J. Paul Getty Museum, and Dr. David Whitehouse, executive director of The Corning Museum of Glass. Their work over many years has led to an exceptional assemblage of rare and beautiful works of glass art, giving us a new appreciation for a material that we so often take for granted in our everyday lives. We thank our colleagues at other institutions throughout the United States and Europe who have generously lent their objects to this exhibition.

Acknowledgments

Karol Wight
Curator of Antiquities, The J. Paul Getty Museum

David Whitehouse
Executive Director, The Corning Museum of Glass

THIS EXHIBITION presents ancient works and modern imitations. Many of these objects are from the collection of The Corning Museum of Glass, and others were borrowed from individuals and museums in the United States and Europe. We thank our colleagues for their generosity in lending such rare and fragile works to this exhibition:

Marino Barovier, Venice.
The British Museum, London: Neil MacGregor, Trevor Coughlan, and Dyfri Williams.
Iris and B. Gerald Cantor Center for Visual Arts at Stanford University, Stanford, California: Thomas Seligman and Jennifer McKenna.
Getty Research Institute, Los Angeles: Thomas Crow and Susan Allen.
Dinah Hulet, McKinleyville, California.
Iparművészeti Múzeum (Museum of Applied Arts), Budapest: Imre Takács and Ágnes Naszlady.
Kölnisches Stadtmuseum, Cologne: Werner Schäfke and Bettina Mosler.
Kunsthistorisches Museum, Vienna: Kurt Gschwantler.
MAK – Austrian Museum of Applied Arts/Contemporary Art, Vienna: Peter Noever and Kathrin Pokorny-Nagel.
The Metropolitan Museum of Art, New York: Philippe de Montebello, Carlos Picón, and Jesse McNab.
Museé des Arts Décoratifs, Paris: Jean-Luc Olivié and Beatrice Salmon.
Museo del Vetro, Murano: Giandomenico Romanelli.
Museum Kunst Palast, Düsseldorf: Helmut Ricke.
Römisch-Germanisches Museum, Cologne: Friederike Naumann-Steckner and Hansgerd Hellenkemper.
Smithsonian American Art Museum, Washington, D.C.: Allison Fenn.
Mark Taylor and David Hill, Quarley, Hampshire, United Kingdom.
Victoria and Albert Museum, London: Mark Jones, Rebecca Wallace, and Reino Liefkes.
Josef Welzel, Hadamar, Germany.
Yale University Art Gallery, New Haven, Connecticut: Susan Matheson and Lynne Addison.
Rainer Zietz, London.

We also acknowledge the dedication of the staff responsible for mounting this exhibition and preparing this catalog at the Getty Villa and The Corning Museum of Glass:

Getty Villa

Department of Antiquities: Carrie Tovar and David Saunders.
Antiquities Conservation: Jerry Podany, Erik Risser, McKenzie Lowry, B. J. Farrar, and David Armendariz.
Editorial: Sahar Tchaitchian.
Education: Ann Steinsapir and Rainer Mack.
Exhibition Design: Merritt Price, Robert Checci, Emily Morishita, and Andrew Pribuss.
Exhibitions: Quincy Houghton and Liz Andres.
Getty Conservation Institute: Marc Walton.
Interactive Programs: Alison Glazier.
Preparations: Bruce Metro, Kevin Marshall, Alfonso Aguilar, Marcus Adams, and Justin Lowman.
Villa Registrar's Office: Sally Hibbard and Jacqueline Cabrera.

The Corning Museum of Glass

Conservation: Stephen Koob.
Curatorial Department: Dedo von Kerssenbrock-Krosigk and Laura Cotton.
Education: Amy Schwartz.
Exhibition Design: Robert Cassetti and Brian Jones.
Librarians: Gail Bardhan, Beth Hylen, and John Bunkley.
Photography: Nicholas Williams, Andrew Fortune, and Allison von Hagn.
Preparators: Joseph Maio, Stephen Hazlett, and Lekova Giadom.
Publications: Richard Price and Jacolyn Saunders.
Registrar's Office: Warren Bunn, Brandy Harold, Lesley Murphy, and Melissa White.
Rights and Reproductions: Jill Thomas-Clark and Mary Chervenak.
The Studio: William Gudenrath.

INTRODUCTION

David Whitehouse
Executive Director, The Corning Museum of Glass

WE OFTEN THINK—rightly—of the 19th century as an age of progress, with numerous advances in the fields of science and technology, manufacturing, and public education. But as far as art and architecture are concerned, it was also an age of revivals. In some cases, the revival of a past vocabulary of design reflected a desire to express or redefine national identity (as with the Celtic Revival in Ireland), while in other cases artists and craftsmen looked back to what they regarded as purer or more natural forms of expression (as with the Pre-Raphaelite Brotherhood in England).

In Europe, this enthusiasm for past or exotic styles led to experiments with visual languages such as Orientalism (the love of images based on the art, architecture, and landscapes of the Islamic world of northern Africa and the Near East), and *Japonisme* (the borrowing of images and aesthetic ideas from Japan, especially after that country opened its ports to foreign trade as a result of the Treaty of Kanagawa in 1854), and to the revival of medieval Gothic architecture and ornament (for example, in the House of Lords, London, which was hailed as "the finest specimen of Gothic civil architecture in Europe" when it opened in 1847).

It is not surprising, therefore, that glassmakers in 19th-century Europe reproduced a wide variety of historical styles, and these are represented by 24 objects in the first section of the catalog (on pages 84–115). Catalog no. **1** is a Roman beaker of the first century A.D., which was blown inside a silver beaker. It was found in Italy in 1865, and it entered The British Museum in 1870. **3** is one of a small number of copies of the beaker, which were made in Italy, probably after the object was published in 1879. **4** is an elegant imitation of a Roman cinerary urn (cf. **2**), made by the Compagnia di Venezia e Murano (C.V.M.) about 1881.

5 is another product of the Compagnia di Venezia e Murano: a replica of a celebrated bowl in the Treasury of San Marco, Venice, that bears enameled, silver-stained, and gilded decoration and was made in the Byzantine Empire (probably at Constantinople) in the 10th century.

6–9 are late 19th-century versions of exotic objects from the Islamic world: two lamps, a vase, and a beaker. **6** was decorated by Philippe-Joseph Brocard (1831–1896), a Paris-based craftsman who produced replicas of medieval Islamic mosque lamps and other pieces that sometimes left the viewer wondering whether an object was original or a copy. A far more prominent French manufacturer, Emile Gallé (1846–1904), produced **7**: a tour de force of glassmaking that combines acid-etched, stained, iridized, enameled, and gilded decoration.

10–14 are versions of late medieval vessels. One of them, a copy of a German or Swiss *Stangenglas* (**14**), was made at the Rheinische Glashütten A.G. at Ehrenfeld, near Cologne, which specialized in replicas and imitations of antique glasses.

15–19 are 19th-century copies of 15th- and 16th-century Venetian originals. **15** is a replica of the *Coppa Barovier*, a celebrated marriage goblet of the 15th century and one of the treasures of the Museo del Vetro, Murano. The maker, the Compagnia di Venezia e Murano, exhibited a similar replica at the world's fair in Paris in 1878. **19** is an aquamanile in the form of a boat, made in Venice by Salviati and Company about 1870. A chronicler, Martin Sanudo, noted that he saw boat-shaped vessels at the Fair of the Ascension in Venice in 1525.

Venetian glass was highly sought-after between the 16th and 18th centuries, and glassmakers in many parts of Europe produced tableware and display objects *à la façon de Venise* (in the manner of Venice). **20** and **21** are two *façon de Venise* goblets made in Hamburg, Germany, by a brilliant flameworker, C. H. F. Müller (1845–1912), whose late 19th-century imitations of 17th-century originals (like Brocard's imitations of mosque lamps) sometimes confounded the experts.

Finally, **22–25** are imitations of Renaissance and later enameled glass from central Europe, and **26** is a mid-19th-century version of a gold ruby goblet made about 100 years earlier.

The following pages focus on just one source of inspiration that stimulated 19th-century glassmakers: the glass of ancient Rome. Five chapters of the book, and five sections of the exhibition, focus on the rediscovery of certain types of Roman glass and their effect on 19th-century glassmaking. The chapters describe cameo glass (**27–46**), gold glass (**47–57**), mosaic glass (**58–79**), cage cups (**80–91**), and historicizing glasses made at Ehrenfeld and Mainz, Germany.

The last two chapters of the book describe the different techniques used to make Roman and 19th-century cameo glass blanks, as well as the present-day reproduction of Roman vessels and what it can teach us about ancient techniques of glassworking.

~:~

I am grateful to my colleagues who contributed to the various sections of this book: William Gudenrath, resident adviser of The Studio of The Corning Museum of Glass; Mark Taylor and David Hill of Roman Glassmakers, Quarley, Hampshire, U.K.; Dr. Karol Wight, curator of antiquities, The J. Paul Getty Museum, Malibu, California; and Dr. Dunja Zobel-Klein, archeologist and art historian, Landesmuseum Mainz, and Dr. Michael J. Klein, head of the Department of Archeology, Landesmuseum Mainz.

Cameo Glass

David Whitehouse

CAMEOS ARE OBJECTS with two or more layers of different colors. The outer layer or layers are partly removed to create decoration in low relief on a background of contrasting color. The first cameo glass vessels were made by the Romans between the late first century B.C. and the early first century A.D. A handful of cameo glasses were produced by Roman glassworkers in the fourth century A.D., a greater number were made by craftsmen in the Islamic world between the ninth and 11th centuries, and Chinese glass cutters in and after the 18th century made more cameo glass than all of their predecessors combined. Nevertheless, cameo glass was comparatively scarce before the late 19th century, when glassmakers in the Stourbridge area of central England produced tens of thousands of objects for consumption at home and abroad.

Roman Cameo Glass

Lapidaries (cutters of precious and semiprecious stones) created hard stone cameos by exploiting the natural layers of decorative minerals such as onyx. They cut the decoration in one or more layers and used the lowest layer as the background. This technique, pioneered in the Hellenistic period, was continued by the lapidaries of the early Roman Empire, who made such masterpieces as the Gemma Augustea and the Gemma Tiberiana. The production of ambitious hard stone gems declined after the mid-first century A.D., but it was revived to some extent in the later Roman Empire.

The Romans also exploited the carefully contrived layering of glass objects with one or more overlays. Glassmakers were able to control the contours and thickness of the glass, which was impossible with even the most carefully selected stones, and they could supply lapidaries with combinations of colors and thicknesses that do not occur in nature. This practice, however, was never common. Indeed, to the best of our knowledge, small objects apart, the Romans made cameo glasses in only two periods: during the reign of Augustus (27 B.C.–A.D. 14) and his immediate successors, and in the fourth century. The earlier group includes some of the first ancient glass objects to attract attention in modern times; the later group was virtually unknown until the 20th century.

The earlier group consists of both vessels and flat objects such as plaques and medallions. It is generally believed that most of the vessels were formed by blowing (see page 61), while the flat objects were cast in two or more layers. The most common combination of colors is opaque white over transparent deep blue, but occasionally transparent green and purple, as well as opaque red, were employed. After the object had been annealed (cooled gradually to room temperature), it was entrusted to the decorator (in all probability, a craftsman skilled in cutting precious stones), who used cutting and grinding wheels and hand tools to remove parts of the overlay(s) to create decoration in low relief.

Fewer than 20 more or less complete early Roman cameo glass vessels are known to exist. The most celebrated of these (which is also the most celebrated example of ancient Roman glass) is the Portland Vase, an amphora, now damaged, decorated with figural scenes that have defied interpretation for at least 400 years (**34**). The vase is attributed to the time of Augustus, and it is thought to have been made in Rome, its likely find-place (see below). An exquisite bottle, known as the Seasons Vase, was also found in Rome, as were numerous fragments. No fewer than three vessels—the Auldjo Jug (**28**) and the Blue Vase, both of which are noted below, and a dipper—and two plaques have been recovered from the ruins of Pompeii. It seems likely, therefore, that many early Roman cameo glass vessels (perhaps the majority) were made in Italy.

Many of these vessels were produced for drinking or dispensing wine, and scenes associated with Bacchus, the god of wine, are common (**29**). The finest of these objects are decorated with great skill, and it is not unreasonable to regard them as luxury items: sought-after in Roman times and, fragments apart, rarities today.

The Rediscovery of Roman Cameo Glass

The Portland Vase was the first glass vessel to attract the admiration of students and collectors of ancient art. The earliest known record of the vase dates from the winter of 1600–1601, when the Provençal polymath Nicolas-Claude Fabri de Peiresc (1580–1637) saw it in the collection of Cardinal Francesco Maria Borbone Del Monte in Rome (Painter and Whitehouse 1990b, pp. 24–28). Del Monte had intended to change his will and leave the vase to Gaston de France (1608–1660), duke of Orléans and brother of King Louis XIII of France, but he died before doing this, and the vase passed to one of his heirs, Alessandro Del Monte. Three months later, Alessandro sold the vase to the future Cardinal Francesco Barberini, after which it remained in the Barberini family for more than 150 years.

The first formal publication of the Portland Vase was in Girolamo Teti's *Aedes Barberinae* (1642). Teti described the vase and conjectured that it once held the ashes of Emperor Severus Alexander, but he had nothing to say about its find-place. In 1697, in *Gli antichi sepolchri*, Pietro-Santi Bartoli stated that the vase had been found in a sarcophagus in a monumental tomb known as the Monte del Grano, a few miles from Rome. According to the minutes of the Consiglio Comunale of Rome, dated May 4, 1582, a subcommittee was appointed to consider acquiring a sarcophagus that had recently been found in the Monte del Grano. The minutes do not refer to the vase. Neither does Flaminio Vacca's *Memorie di varie antichità trovate in diversi luoghi della Città di Roma*, which was written in 1594 (but not published until 1771). However, it describes the discovery of the sarcophagus, which was already believed to be that of Severus Alexander and his mother, Julia Mamaea. Therefore, Bartoli, writing more than 100 years after the opening of the Monte del Grano, may have been mistaken, and we may never know exactly where or when the vase was found. We are certain, though, that it was in Rome, and attracted attention, in 1600–1601.

We are much better informed about the history of the Portland Vase after it was acquired by the Barberini family. At least 14 drawings of the vase, made in the early 17th century, survive. All of them were probably created by artists contributing to the *Museum Chartaceum* (Paper Museum), an enormous project to document antiquities of all kinds, organized by Cassiano dal Pozzo, the Barberinis' librarian. By the mid-18th century, the fortunes of the Barberinis had declined, and after losing heavily at cards, Princess Cordelia Barberini-Colonna sold the Portland Vase to James Byres, a Scotsman living in Rome. Byres then sold it to Sir William Hamilton, the British ambassador to the court of Naples, who took it to England in 1783. The following year, Hamilton sold the vase to the dowager duchess of Portland, in whose family it remained until the seventh duke of Portland sold it to The British Museum in London. From the moment it arrived in England, the vase attracted considerable attention, and the master potter Josiah Wedgwood invested several years of time and effort in producing his first ceramic replica (**32**).

The second example of Roman cameo glass to attract the interest of antiquarians was the bottle that is generally known as the "Vase des saisons" (Seasons Vase). The early history of this object involves two of the characters who played roles in the drama of the Portland Vase: Peiresc and the duke of Orléans.

Like dal Pozzo, but on a smaller scale, Peiresc assembled a collection of drawings of antiquities, which is now in the Bibliothèque Nationale, Paris. Among the drawings is a watercolor showing three views of an object that is immediately recognizable as the Seasons Vase. An index of Peiresc's archive, compiled in 1635, unequivocally describes this drawing and shows that the object had been discovered in or before that year. The approximate date of the discovery is recorded in two letters written by Peiresc in 1633. In a letter to Denys Guillaumin, Peiresc described a "*larmoir* [tear bottle] in the collection of Monsieur, brother of the king, which is of blue enamel embellished with white cameo figures." In the second letter, addressed to Claude Menestrier, librarian to Cardinal Francesco Barberini, he wrote: "Furthermore, two other ancient vases have been discovered . . . [one belongs to M. Sourdis]; the other is of blue glass with only three cameo figures in milk white glass, like [the cameo glass] of Cardinal Del Monte, which now belongs to your most eminent patron. . . . It is said that the enamel [vase] came from Rome" (cited in Guibert 1910, pp. 64–65).

Rome was also the find-place of the next ancient Roman cameo glass to attract attention: the Carpegna Cameo. This is a plaque decorated with a scene that shows Dionysus appearing to Ariadne on the island of Naxos. The cameo was found, allegedly in (or near?) the Catacomb of Priscilla in Rome, in the late 17th century. It was described first by Filippo Buonarotti in 1698, when it was in the collection of Cardinal Gaspare Carpegna (d. 1714). Later, it belonged to the Vatican Library, and it was taken to Paris in 1797.

Thus, by 1700, three outstanding examples of Roman cameo glass had come to light (all apparently in or near Rome) and were the subjects of antiquarian research.

The rediscovery and exploration of Pompeii and Herculaneum, two cities destroyed by the eruption of Vesuvius in A.D. 79, uncovered an unprecedented quantity of Roman antiquities, from works of art to objects of daily use. Two outstanding examples of cameo glass were discovered at Pompeii in the 1830s: the Auldjo Jug and the Blue Vase.

The Auldjo Jug (**28**) was found between 1830 and 1832 in the House of the Faun, an opulent residence that contained, in addition to the bronze statue of a faun, the Alexander Mosaic, one of the most celebrated works of art that have come down to us from antiquity.

The Blue Vase, the largest and most richly decorated Roman cameo glass, is said to have been found in 1837 in a tomb attached to the House of the Mosaic Columns. The object is remarkable. It is an amphora that is larger than any other surviving cameo glass vessel. The body is covered with elaborate decoration consisting of exuberant vine scrolls and cupids playing musical instruments and treading grapes. Although it is clear that the Blue Vase was found in or before 1837, the circumstances of its discovery are obscure. The vase was revealed on December 29, 1837, when King Ferdinand II visited the excavations at Pompeii. In an elaborate charade, previously opened tombs were filled with treasures and reopened to delight the royal visitor. We have no idea, therefore, of the actual find-place of the Blue Vase.

When Apsley Pellatt, a leading London glassmaker, published an influential collection of essays titled *Curiosities of Glass Making* (**31**) in 1849, he illustrated three Roman cameo glasses on the title page: the Portland Vase, the Auldjo Jug, and the Blue Vase. These three objects created a fascination for cameo glass.

19th-Century Imitations

In modern times, the manufacture of cameo glass reached its greatest height in England and France in the second half of the 19th century. In England, George Woodall supervised the carving of elaborate historicizing scenes that showcased his extraordinary technical ability. In France, Emile Gallé directed a workshop that produced remarkable glasses carved and engraved from blanks with a bewildering array of overlays consisting of trails, blobs, and pads of colored glass, as well as metallic inclusions.

The story of modern European imitations of cameo glass begins, however, in the early 19th century—possibly as early as 1804—when glassmakers in Bohemia began to case colorless glass objects with a layer of colored glass that was then selectively cut through to create a design by revealing the base glass. By 1836, these glassmakers were producing vessels with two or more overlays. Their work attracted attention in Britain and the United States. The English firm of W. H., B. & J. Richardson exhibited blue, green, and red cased glass at a Manchester trade fair in 1845–1846, and the April 1846 issue of the *Art-Union* magazine reported that "Messrs. Richardson are directing considerable attention to the improvement of coloured glass; in this art we yet lag behind our neighbours; . . . these gentlemen have, however, already made great advance in rivaling the productions of Bohemia; and we have little doubt that, a few years hence, we shall see at least [the] equal [of] the best of the imported articles . . ." (Hajdamach 1991, p. 82).

The early years of English cameo glass making were dominated by John Northwood (1836–1902). In 1860, John and his brother, Joseph, opened a finishing shop in Wordsley known as J. & J. Northwood. Joseph managed the business, while John developed new decorating techniques. In 1861, John invented the Template Etching Machine, which decorated objects mechanically by tracing the design in their wax-coated surfaces before they were exposed to hydrofluoric acid. Four years later, he introduced an improved etching machine, and later he developed "white acid," a mixture of hydrofluoric acid and potassium carbonate or sodium carbonate, which enabled him to decorate an object from start to finish by etching alone.

At the same time, John Northwood established his reputation as an outstanding engraver. His Elgin Vase, completed in 1863, is a colorless glass amphora engraved with horses and riders, inspired by the Elgin Marbles in The British Museum. The vase was hailed as a masterpiece, and it paved the way for the "rock crystal" style of high-relief English cut glass.

Northwood's skills as an etcher and engraver led to his triumphant replica of the Portland Vase (**33**). Impressed by the Elgin Vase, Philip Pargeter (1826–1906) of the Red House Glass Works (Wordsley) told Northwood, "I believe I can make the Portland Vase if you can decorate it" (Beard 1956, p. 6). Northwood accepted the challenge. The blank was blown at the Red House Glass Works in 1873, and Northwood spent the next three years decorating it. In his reminiscences, Thomas Woodall (whom we will meet shortly) recalled assisting Northwood in decorating the vase: "I made the first drawing and painted the resist for acidizing this out, which was a fairly long job as it was fairly thick in [the] outer coating to get the necessary relief. Mr. John Northwood than [*sic*] took it in hand for carving with steel points and the engravers lathe he used a little" (Haden 1993, p. 43).

Northwood was not the only skilled carver of cameo glasses in the Stourbridge area. Joseph Locke (1846–1936) was another. After joining Hodgetts, Richardson and Son in Wordsley, Locke learned the cameo technique from a French engraver, Alphonse Lechevrel (1850–1924), who spent just two years (1877–1879) with the company (Grover and Grover 1980, p. 3). When the firm decided to participate in the Paris world's fair of 1878, Locke was persuaded to follow Northwood's precedent and carve a replica of the Portland Vase. Although it was unfinished, Locke's vase (**35**) occupied a prominent place in the exhibit and won a silver medal.

The manufacture of cameo glass in England reached its zenith between about 1880 and 1900. John Northwood was the catalyst. In 1881, he was appointed artistic director of Stevens & Williams, a Stourbridge firm that specialized in decorated glassware. Under Northwood's leadership, Stevens & Williams produced cameo glass in a wide range of shapes and colors throughout the 1880s, sometimes decorating pieces on the premises and sometimes farming them out to J. & J. Northwood.

At that time, another local company, Thomas Webb & Sons of the Dennis Glass Works in Amblecote, rivaled—and later eclipsed—Stevens & Williams in the production of cameo glass. Founded in 1837, the Webb firm flourished under the direction of Thomas Wilkes Webb (1837–1891). In 1878, the catalog of the Paris world's fair described the Webb company as "the best makers of Crystal Glass in England and consequently, in the world." In the 27 years during which Thomas Wilkes Webb ran the firm, the Dennis Glass Works produced more than 10,000 designs, an average of more than one a day!

Webb employed some of the most talented glass engravers of the day, recruiting them not only in England but also in Ireland, France, and Bohemia. None, however, was superior to George Woodall (1850–1925), his brother Thomas (1849–1926), and the members of their team (**41**).

By the late 1880s, cameo glass was extremely fashionable. Webb employed every available engraver to work overtime, and the Woodall team expanded until it numbered about 70 members. The team took several shortcuts to speed production. They made extensive use of acid etching to remove unwanted glass, and they made greater use than Northwood of the engraver's lathe. They also introduced white overlays with a bluish tinge that, when thinned over brown or burgundy base glass, allowed them to achieve an extraordinary range of shading (**42** and **43**). The Woodalls' creations included not only neoclassical designs but also an eclectic selection of decoration from printed sources, such as Owen Jones's *Examples of Chinese Ornament* (1867), which inspired *The Great Tazza* (**40**) and *The Great Dish*.

However, the vogue for English cameo glass was short-lived. It had begun to attract attention in the 1870s, and it was still popular in the early 1900s. "No more noble ornament can be conceived in a room than a fine well-designed and artistically executed cameo glass," wrote Owen Jones in *The Pottery Gazette* on January 1, 1908. Nevertheless, just four years later, George Woodall reported that the market for true cameo glass had been ruined by the arrival of inexpensive enameled imitations from the Continent.

The dominant figure in French cameo glass making was Emile Gallé (1846–1904). Gallé, who took over his father's business in Nancy, exhibited at the Paris world's fair of 1878, and in the 1880s he began to make glass with multicolored inclusions (Blount and Blount 1968, p. 17). He exhibited new work in Paris in 1889, including his first multilayered cameo glass. It was highly original, and it was widely acclaimed. Gallé continued to make cameo glass for the rest of his life (**46**). His business, which extended from ceramics and glass to fine furniture, prospered, and in 1900 he had some 300 employees. Today, Gallé's glass is admired for its extraordinary inventiveness, technical virtuosity, and exploration of the nascent Art Nouveau style.

Gallé was by no means the only French manufacturer of cameo glass. His creations inspired Auguste Daum (1853–1909) and his brother, Antonin (1864–1930), to produce cameo glass at their Verrerie de Nancy, and Gallé's former employees, the Müller brothers, made cameo glass at their own factories in Luneville and Croismare. However, just as the virtuoso products of the Woodalls were priced out of the English market shortly after 1900, so, at about the same time, the individual, labor-intensive creations that had made Gallé famous were replaced in France by acid-etched cameo glass made on an industrial scale.

Cameo glasses, clearly inspired by white-over-blue Roman objects such as the Portland Vase, were also made in Italy. They include an amphora with two overlays—white and light blue—decorated by Attilio Spaccarelli in 1891 (**44**) and a bottle with a satyr and a maenad that is attributed to the Compagnia di Venezia e Murano (C.V.M.) in the late 19th century. The object decorated by Spaccarelli resembles an amphora in The Toledo Museum of Art that also features Dionysiac figures (*Cameo Glass* 1982, p. 119, no. 89). A white-over-blue vase in a private collection is signed by "E. Montani [or Montoni], Roma." Evidently, some cameo glass blanks, presumably made on Murano, were decorated in Rome.

Gold Glass

David Whitehouse

THE TERM *gold glass* is usually applied to several types of Hellenistic and Roman objects decorated with designs cut and/or engraved in gold foil that is sandwiched between two fused layers of glass. Hellenistic gold glass was made by sandwiching the decoration between two closely fitting cast, ground, and polished vessels that were then fused (Tatton-Brown and Andrews 1991, pp. 48–49). Many Roman gold glasses apparently were made by applying the gold foil to the surface of a blown object, reheating it, and inflating a parison against the decorated surface, after which the two parisons were tooled and sheared to produce objects—usually dishes and bowls—of the desired shape (*Glass of the Caesars* 1987, pp. 262–268).

The earliest known gold-glass vessels were made in the Hellenistic world between about 300 B.C. and the late second century B.C. These objects have a layer of gold foil, cut into sometimes intricate designs, preserved between inner and outer layers of colorless glass. It is customary to attribute these luxurious objects to Alexandria in Egypt, although the majority of objects with known or assumed findplaces are said to have been found in Italy.

Roman Gold Glasses

A new variety of gold glass came into use in the first century A.D. It consisted of ribbon mosaic glass (which is described on page 35) incorporating strips of gold foil sandwiched between layers of colorless glass. This combination, usually on small perfume bottles and cylindrical boxes decorated with gold and strips of brilliant blue, green, and purple glass, created a jewellike effect of great opulence.

Although we sometimes read that "there was a continuous tradition of the use of gold by glass-workers from the third century BC until the second or early third century AD" (*Glass of the Caesars* 1987, p. 263), the evidence—for gold sandwich glass, at least—is inconclusive. What we do know is that a number of glass objects were decorated on the outside with carefully cut gold-foil ornament. They include a late first-century ewer from the treasure found at Begram, Afghanistan, and a similar vessel in The Corning Museum of Glass (Whitehouse 2001, pp. 273–274, no. 866), the second- to third-century Daphne Ewer and its close parallels from an archeological site in Georgia (*Glass of the Caesars* 1987, p. 273, no. 150; Whitehouse 2001, pp. 266–270, no. 864), and the third- to fourth-century Disch Cantharus (**47**) and its lost counterpart (*Glass of the Caesars* 1987, pp. 253–254, no. 143; Whitehouse 2001, pp. 275–277, no. 867). There are other examples of fourth-century glass objects decorated on the outside with gold foil, notably a cup with scenes from the Old Testament, in the Römisch-Germanisches Museum, Cologne (*Glass of the Caesars* 1987, pp. 25–27, no. 5). One of these objects decorated with unprotected gold, the Disch Cantharus, was copied, somewhat freely, in the late 19th century (**52**; see below).

Roman glassworkers resumed sandwiching decorated gold foil between layers of fused glass in the late second or third century. The earliest objects include medallions decorated with portraits, sometimes accompanied by Greek or Latin inscriptions that identify the subject (*ibid.*, pp. 276–277, nos. 152 and 153). Each medallion consists of a dark blue disk decorated with gold foil that was protected by fusing a disk of colorless glass over the top of the object. The most remarkable feature of these medallions is the way in which facial and other features are suggested by stippling with a fine point. Although some examples of this group have been denounced as modern forgeries, it seems clear that the majority belong to the second and third centuries and represent an otherwise little-known genre of miniature Roman portraiture.

Also attributed to the third century is a group of fragmentary vessels with inscriptions made of gilded rods (e.g., **48**). The inscriptions decorate the floor of open vessels blown from two gathers. Individual letters were formed from thin (D. not more than 1 mm) rods of colorless glass. The rods were softened in a flame, bent into the desired shapes, and gilded. They were then arranged on the parison that was intended to form the base of the vessel. A second parison was inflated over the inscription, sandwiching it between the two layers. The top and bottom parts of the vessel were then given their final shape.

In the fourth century, two new types of blown gold sandwich glass came into use. The first type, which is represented by fragments of a bowl found in a cemetery in Cologne, Germany, and by many fragments from known and unknown sites in Italy and other parts of Europe, comprises colorless open forms decorated on the outside with small gold-foil motifs that were covered with flattened blobs of blue or green glass. Seen from inside the vessel, the decoration consists of small elements depicted in gold on a dark blue or dark green background. The bowl from Cologne was found in a grave of the second half of the fourth century (*Glass of the Caesars* 1987, pp. 277–279, no. 154).

The second type of fourth-century gold glass is very much more common. It consists of the bases of dishes or bowls decorated at the center with medallions sandwiched between two layers of colorless glass (*ibid.*, pp. 265–268). The medallions contain a wide variety of subject matter: biblical scenes, Christ and the saints, Jewish subjects, legends, pagan deities, individual portraits, portraits of couples and families, and animals. Many of the medallions are surrounded by inscriptions, and these indicate that the decoration was intended to be viewed from the inside of the vessel (**49** and **50**).

No complete vessel survives. Instead, nearly all known examples are the bases of objects carefully trimmed to form roundels slightly larger than the gilded medallions, and these were frequently attached to the walls of Christian and (less often) Jewish catacombs outside Rome and (much less often) to the walls of catacombs in other Roman cities of Italy.

None of these medallions can be dated closely on archeological grounds, even when the exact find-place is known. It is possible, however, that some of the inscriptions refer to prominent individuals, such as Pope Damasus (r. 366–384) and Memmius Vitrasius Orfitus, who was prefect of Rome between 354 and 359. In any case, it is generally accepted that most gold glasses of this type were made in the fourth century.

The Rediscovery of Roman Gold Glasses

The catacombs of Rome never ceased to attract attention, and they are mentioned in numerous medieval documents, even in the accounts of Muslim writers. The catacombs and their contents became the subject of serious antiquarian study in the late 16th century. The first publication of gold-glass medallions from the catacombs was Antonio Bosio's *Roma sotteranea* (Subterranean Rome), which appeared posthumously in 1632 and contained engravings of six examples. A further six examples of medallions appeared in Paolo Aringhi's *Roma subterranea novissima* (Latest [finds from] subterranean Rome), which was published in Rome in 1651. The number of known examples of gold-glass medallions from the catacombs increased steadily in the second half of the 17th century, and in 1716, when Filippo Buonarotti published his *Osservazioni sopra alcuni frammenti di vasi antichi di vetro ornati de figure trovati nei cimiteri di Roma* (Observations on several fragments of ancient glass vessels decorated with figures found in the cemeteries of Rome), he was able to include no fewer than 72 specimens. Four years later, in his *Osservazioni sopra i cimiterj dei santi martiri ed antichi cristiani di Roma* (Observations on the cemeteries of the holy martyrs and ancient Christians of Rome), Marco Antonio Boldetti added 28 hitherto unpublished gold glasses, bringing the number of published examples to about 100. Among the objects published by Boldetti was a more or less complete bowl decorated with a gold-glass medallion: the first demonstration that the medallions were fragments from vessels.

In the 19th century, the leading scholar of gold-glass studies was a Jesuit priest, Raffaele Garrucci, who in 1858 published the first edition of *Vetri ornati di figure in oro trovati nei cimiteri dei cristiani primitivi di Roma* (Glasses decorated with figures in gold found in the Christian cemeteries of Rome; **51**). Garrucci's publication included no fewer than 380 gold glasses, mostly medallions from the catacombs of Rome. A second edition of his book appeared in 1864, followed by his monumental *Storia dell'arte cristiana* (History of Christian art; 1880, 1886), the third volume of which included a survey of gold glasses. Garrucci was not the only 19th-century scholar to focus on gold glasses from the catacombs. Giambattista De Rossi also published widely on early Christian antiquities, including gold glasses, and he was the first person to describe a medallion depicting an unambiguously Jewish subject. Garrucci's publications, however, reached a wider audience, and they came to the attention of glassmakers on Murano at just the moment when historicism was enjoying an enormous vogue. It is not surprising, therefore, that gold glasses now entered the repertoire of Muranese glassmaking.

The last substantial 19th-century study of gold glasses from the catacombs was by Hermann Vopel, who, in *Die altchristlichen Goldgläser* (Early Christian gold glasses; 1899), provided an up-to-date catalog of finds and attempted to place these objects in their correct chronological sequence. This was an impressive scholarly venture, but for glassmakers on Murano, the principal—perhaps the only—source of inspiration was the publications of Garrucci.

Early Forgeries of Gold Glasses

In the mid-18th century, the great French antiquarian Anne Claude Philippe Caylus (1692–1765) reported that dealers in Rome were selling imitations of gold glasses, which they passed off to tourists as antiquities (Caylus 1752–1767, v. 3, pp. 193–205).

As far as I am aware, none of the forgeries mentioned by Caylus has been identified, but an apparently somewhat later group of forgeries, also from Rome, has attracted scholarly attention. These objects consist of fragments of ancient glass vessels with modern painted and gilded decoration, assembled as sandwiches in a rather distant imitation of gold-glass medallions. The decoration, which is poorly executed, includes Christian figures and Latin inscriptions, some of which contain errors (such as "PARCE VOBISCO" for PAX VOBISCVM: Whitehouse 2003, pp. 108–109, no. 1066). Gustavus A. Eisen (1927, v. 2, pp. 571–581) published a group of these objects and attributed them to the period between the third and sixth centuries. These objects, however, had long been recognized as forgeries. Eisen himself recorded the information that helps us to pinpoint where and when they were made. He wrote: "Of the thirty specimens of this series known to the author, twenty-two or more belonged once in the collection of Count Bartholomeo [*sic*] Borghesi. . . . According to him they were found in the Catacombs of Rome in 1849, a time when . . . the finder of antiques could dispose of them as he pleased without restrictions" (*ibid.*, p. 573).

Objects from this collection were offered to The British Museum in London in 1909. They failed to impress O. M. Dalton of the Department of British and Medieval Antiquities, who decided that they had "all the appearance of being false." Dalton's opinion has been reinforced by every student of ancient glass—except Eisen.

Bartolomeo Borghesi (1781–1860) was not a member of the princely Borghese family, but he was one of the founders of Roman epigraphy. Indeed, when Theodor

Mommsen published his groundbreaking *Inscriptiones Regni Neapolitani* (Inscriptions of the kingdom of Naples; 1852), he dedicated it to Borghesi, addressing him as "magistro, patrono, amico" (master, patron, friend).

The identification of Bartolomeo Borghesi as the first known owner of gold glasses of this type establishes that many of them were made in or before 1860, the year of Borghesi's death. Unfortunately, this does not help us to establish where they were made, apart from indicating that they are almost certainly Italian. The objects have been assumed to be Venetian, but since their manufacture involved neither fusing nor enameling, there is no reason to suppose that they were made by glassworkers. I suspect that they were cobbled together in Rome for unscrupulous dealers.

19th-Century Imitations of Gold Glasses

Venetian glassmakers began to imitate ancient gold glasses in the 1870s. They were not making forgeries, but drawing on Roman prototypes to inspire modern revivals of an ancient theme. The leading exponent of this revival was Francesco Toso Borella (1846–1905), a prominent decorator. In 1873, he donated an example of his enameling to the Museo Vetrario (now the Museo del Vetro), Murano, and, beginning in 1888, he won national and international prizes. The Museo del Vetro also owns gold glasses that are known to be the work of Toso Borella, donated by his son. The principal source of the designs used by Toso Borella to decorate his gold glasses was probably the monographs published by Garrucci in 1858 (**51**), 1864, and 1876.

Other Muranese manufacturers of gold glasses included the Compagnia di Venezia e Murano (C.V.M.), which began to produce them under the direction of the celebrated Roman goldsmith Alessandro Castellani (1824–1883). Castellani began to advise the company in 1878, and, at the Paris world's fair of that same year, it exhibited a bowl of smoky, almost colorless glass decorated with a large central medallion, as well as six smaller medallions on bottle-green backgrounds.

Very few Roman vessels decorated with unprotected gold were imitated in the 19th century. The most notable example is the Disch Cantharus (**47**), which takes its name from one of its first owners, the collector Charles Damien Disch. The object came to light in Cologne in 1864, and imitations were made in both Italy and Germany. The Compagnia di Venezia e Murano exhibited a rather crude version of the cantharus at the Paris world's fair in 1878 (Barovier Mentasti 1982, p. 210), and a drawing of another replica appears in a manuscript depicting the same company's products in or about 1895 (Lanmon and Whitehouse 1993, p. 137, fig. 49.3; for the date, see Liefkes 1994, p. 321). Imitations of the Disch Cantharus (**52**) were also published in two of the catalogs (1881, 1886 [**109**]) of the Rheinische Glashütten A.G. in Ehrenfeld, Germany (see pages 41–45 and Schäfke 1979, pp. 83 and 169). It is intriguing to note that the first Muranese versions of the vessel were produced three years before its first recorded publication (Aus'm Weerth 1881, p. 121, no. 1356).

Cage Cups

David Whitehouse

CAGE CUPS are vessels with three-dimensional openwork decoration. The great majority of ancient cage cups were made in the fourth century A.D., although several of them (such as a bucket in the Treasury of San Marco, Venice; see below) are said to be somewhat later. The forms of late Roman cage cups are varied. In fact, some of them are not cups at all and could not have functioned as drinking vessels. They include not only beakers (such as **82**), some of which are inscribed with Greek or Latin toasts, confirming that they were indeed intended for drinking, but also bowl-shaped vessels (such as **81**), some of which were lamps, buckets, dishes, and perhaps an amphora (*Glass of the Caesars* 1987, pp. 185–186; Whitehouse 1993).

The term *cage cup* is derived from the presence on most examples of an openwork "cage" or "net" composed of rows of contiguous circular or nearly circular meshes. In their classic study of the Rothschild Lycurgus Cup (**80**) and other cage cups, Donald B. Harden and Jocelyn M. C. Toynbee divided cage cups into two groups: those with figural decoration, with or without a cage and inscription, and those with cages but not figures, with or without inscriptions (Harden and Toynbee 1959). The figures, cages, and inscriptions are attached to the wall of the vessels by narrow struts or "bridges." Most cage cups are monochrome (usually colorless, and occasionally dichroic), but some have two or even three colored overlays.

Despite a vigorous debate in recent years, it seems almost certain that the entire cage cup—body, bridges, and cage—was created by carving a thick-walled blank with wheels and hand-held tools. The alternative view, that cage cups were made by forcing molten glass into a mold, seems to be contradicted by the clear signs of cold working on objects whose surface is well preserved, and by the difficulty of imagining how a multicolored cage cup, such as the Trivulzio Cage Cup (see page 26), could have been formed in this manner. (For additional discussion of this idea, see pages 30–31.) It appears far more reasonable to suppose that Roman cage cups, such as the beaker with a cage and an inscription from Daruvar, Croatia (**82**), and the Lycurgus Cup, were decorated by cold working, in much the same way as their 20th-century replicas were decorated by Fritz W. Schäfer (**88**) and Josef Welzel (**89**).

Ancient cage cups or fragments of cage cups have been found in many parts of the Roman Empire, from Britain to the Near East, and even beyond the imperial frontier. While most cage cups were made in the fourth century, a few vessels with openwork decoration were produced in the first century, notably a beaker from Nijmegen in the Netherlands and the famous Lighthouse Beaker from Begram, Afghanistan (Koster and Whitehouse 1989).

The Rediscovery of Roman Cage Cups

At least one Roman cage cup probably remained aboveground throughout late antiquity and the Middle Ages. This is the bucket-shaped object in the Treasury of San Marco, Venice, which is made of transparent pale green glass and is decorated with an openwork hunting scene and a cage consisting of four rows of meshes (Harden and Toynbee 1959, p. 204, no. 3). Although the bucket is not listed in the medieval inventories of the contents of the Treasury, it is generally assumed that it was part of the booty from the sack of Constantinople in 1204. In any case, the first publication of the bucket appears to be by Antonio Pasini in *Il tesoro di San Marco* (Venice: F. Ongania, 1885–1886, p. 100), long after the publication of the Trivulzio Cage Cup.

Indeed, the Trivulzio Cage Cup, which is now one of the treasures of the Civiche Raccolte Archeologiche in Milan, Italy (*Glass of the Caesars* 1987, pp. 238–239, no. 134), was the first Roman cage cup to attract attention in modern times. The object, which takes its name from the 18th-century Milanese collector Carlo Trivulzio, who acquired it in 1777, is a beaker with a colorless body and green, blue, and light brown openwork. A Latin inscription in green—"BIBE VIVAS MVLTIS ANNIS" (Drink! May you live for many years)—surrounds the rim, and the body of the vessel is enclosed in a blue and brown cage consisting of four concentric rings of meshes.

Thanks to the research of Dr. Elisabetta Roffia (1993, pp. 184–197), we now know that the Trivulzio Cage Cup was found in 1675 in a marble sarcophagus at Mandella, near Novara. It was acquired by Eriprando Visconti, a member of the family that had ruled Milan for centuries, and it eventually came into the hands of Carlo Trivulzio.

The Trivulzio Cage Cup became famous because it appears in the notes added to the Italian translation of Johann Joachim Winckelmann's groundbreaking study, *Geschichte der Kunst des Alterthums* (History of art in antiquity), published in 1764. In the first Italian edition of Winckelmann's classic, which was published in Milan in 1779, the translators and commentators correctly identified the technique employed to decorate the cup: "né la rete né i caratteri furono saldati in alcun modo, ma il tutto è stato lavorato al torno su una soda massa di vetro freddo colla ruota, nella stessa guisa in cui si fanno i cammei" (Neither the net [i.e., the cage] nor the letters were joined in any way, but the whole [object] was made from a solid mass of cold glass in the same way one makes cameos; Winckelmann 1779, pp. 26–27, n. 5).

Fragments apart, the next discovery of a cage cup was in 1785, when a small bell-shaped cup came to light in a tomb at Daruvar, some 60 miles east-southeast of Zagreb in Croatia. The cup (**82**), which is colorless, has an inscription below the rim and a cage consisting of three rows of meshes. It was published by Luigi Bossi in *Observations sur le vase que l'on conservait à Gênes sous le nom de Sacro Catino* (Observations on the vase, preserved in Genoa, known as the Sacro Catino), Turin: Jean Giossi, 1807, pp. 101–113. Bossi, who likened the object to the Trivulzio Cage Cup, noted that he had acquired it in 1790 and that it had subsequently entered the collection of Prince Johann Sigismund Khevenhüller-Metsch. The date of the discovery of the Daruvar cage cup does not appear in modern literature, but it is recorded in the caption of a print engraved by Montelli after a drawing by Caronni, in the Kunsthistorisches Museum, Vienna: "Fragmentum poculi vitrei inv.[m] prope Opp. Daruvar in Sepulchro apud Monticulum, qua vergit ad Orietem anno MDCCXVC, die 15 Maii" (Fragment of a glass cup found near the town of Daruvar in a tomb in a tumulus that lies to the east, on May 15, 1785).

In 1825, a third cage cup was uncovered. It was found at Strasbourg, France, in a stone sarcophagus that also contained a gold coin of Constans II (r. as caesar from 333 and as emperor from 337 to 350). The object, which appears to have been destroyed in 1870 during the Franco-Prussian War, is known from 19th-century descriptions and illustrations. It was a rather narrow bell-shaped beaker of colorless glass with a green inscription and a red or purple cage. The Latin inscription was incomplete, but it may be restored with confidence as "... MA]XIM[IA]NE AVGV[STE ...," a clear reference to Emperor Maximian (r. 286–310). The inscription establishes that the cage cup was made no later than 310, and the associated coin shows that it was buried no earlier than 333 (Harden and Toynbee 1959, p. 210, no. B10). Reports of a similar cage cup, also lost, which was said to bear the inscription "DIVVS MAXIMIANVS AVGVSTVS" and to have been found at Arles in 1872, are believed to be mistaken (*ibid.*, p. 211, no. C6).

In 1844, two new cage cups were discovered in Cologne, Germany. They were found in two stone sarcophagi in the Roman cemetery in Benesisstrasse. One of these vessels was a colorless bell-shaped beaker with a Greek inscription and a cage consisting of two concentric rows of meshes surrounding a central openwork pattern (*ibid.*, p. 208, no. B1). The inscription was a toast: "ΠΙ]Ε ΖΗCΑΙC ΚΑΛΩ[C" (Drink! May you live well). The sarcophagus in which it was found also contained a coin of Constantine II (r. 337–340). This cage cup, formerly in Berlin (cf. **83**), is believed to have been destroyed in 1945.

The second cage cup found in 1844, now in Munich, is similar to the first one. It is colorless and has an inscription and a cage composed of two concentric rows of meshes and a central openwork pattern (*ibid.*, p. 208, no. B2). The inscription, in Latin, is also a toast: "BIBE MVLTIS ANNIS" (Drink for many years!).

One other cage cup came to the attention of antiquarians at about the same time. This is the Rothschild Lycurgus Cup (Fig. 1 and **80**), a bell-shaped vessel with an openwork frieze representing the death of Lycurgus, a mythical king of the Thracian Edoni, who attacked Dionysus and his followers (*ibid.*, pp. 179–203, no. A1; *Glass*

FIGURE 1
The Rothschild Lycurgus Cup. Roman Empire, fourth century A.D. H. 16.5 cm, D. (rim) 13.2 cm. The British Museum, London (MLA 1958.12-.2.1).

of the Caesars 1987, pp. 245–249, no. 139). One of the maenads (Dionysus's female devotees), Ambrosia, threw a stone at Lycurgus, who tried to seize her. Ambrosia called on Mother Earth to save her. Earth transformed Ambrosia into a vine, which enveloped Lycurgus in its branches. The cup depicts Lycurgus, the vine, and Dionysus and his followers. The openwork decoration is remarkable, and the glass itself is equally extraordinary: the presence of minute quantities of colloidal gold and silver makes the cup dichroic; that is, it is green in reflected light and red when light shines through it.

The first record of the Lycurgus Cup was in 1845, when J. de Witte mentioned it in a footnote to an article by J. Roulez: "Lycurgue furieux," published in *Annali dell'Instituto di Corrispondenza Archeologica*, v. 17, pp. 111–131. De Witte noted, on page 114, that he had seen the cup in Paris "a few years ago," when it was in the hands of a certain M. Dubois. In *Glass of the Caesars* (1987), the first reference to the cup as belonging to the Rothschild family is given as 1862, when Baron Lionel de Rothschild lent it to the South Kensington Museum (now the Victoria and Albert Museum) in London. However, 11 years earlier, it had been illustrated by Delamotte (1851), who described it as already belonging to the baron. The Lycurgus Cup was acquired by The British Museum in 1958.

Imitations and Replicas

A beaker in the Museum of Applied Arts in Budapest, Hungary, may be the first modern imitation of an ancient cage cup (**84**). The beaker, which was blown of colorless glass, has an applied bright blue inscription but no cage. It was designed by Leó Valentin Pantocsek (1812–1893) about 1867.

A decade later, the Compagnia di Venezia e Murano (C.V.M.) produced an imitation of the Strasbourg cage cup, which the company showed at the Paris world's fair of 1878 (**85**). This is not a replica. To compensate for the fact that the original cage cup is not free-standing, the imitation is furnished with a hollow foot. The object was blown from two gathers of colorless glass, and the inscription and cage, both of which are red, were applied. The inscription—"MAXIMIANVS AVGVSTVS"—differs slightly from the inscription on the original and recalls the inscription on the cage cup reputedly found at Arles. The relationship between the Strasbourg cage cup, the reports of the discovery at Arles, and the C.V.M. replica requires further investigation.

The first true replicas of a Roman cage cup were produced in the early 1880s, when a glass workshop in Zwiesel, Germany, made several copies of the beaker in Munich (Kisa 1908, v. 2, p. 619) and at least one variation on the theme: a cover for a tankard, which was exhibited at the Nuremberg trade fair in 1881 or 1882 (Friedrich 1882a, b). The replicas were wheel-cut, and each took about six months to manufacture. They were sold at the Nuremberg fair of 1884. Kisa (1908, v. 2, p. 619, note) implied that another workshop in Bavaria also made copies of the Munich cage cup in 1881. As far as I am aware, the present whereabouts of these replicas are unknown.

The 19th-century replicas of the Munich cage cup seem to have attracted little or no attention in Italy. Nevertheless, several scholars, such as Gerolamo D'Adda in 1870, echoed the opinion of Winckelmann's Italian editors—that cage cups were finished by grinding, cutting, and polishing. In addition, Vincenzo Zanetti, the founder of the Museo Vetrario on Murano (Zecchin 1968, p. 178), was convinced that the leading Muranese glass cutter of the day, Giovanni Albertini, was capable of replicating the object. However, it was not until 1938, when a group of apprentices from Murano visited Milan and examined the Trivulzio Cage Cup, that they accepted Zanetti's opinion. Years later, two of these apprentices, Bepi Fuga and Cesare Barbini, formed and cut on the wheel an imitation of a Roman cage cup: a cup of colorless glass with a colored cage and an inscription that reads "LZ MCMLXIII." "LZ" are the initials of Luigi Zecchin, the distinguished scholar of Venetian glass, and "MCMLXIII" is the Latin equivalent of the date 1963.

In the following year, Fritz W. Schäfer, then a student at the Academy of Fine Arts in Munich, Germany, examined the multicolored Roman cage cup found in the Cologne suburb of Braunsfeld in 1960 (Fig. 2; *Glass of the Caesars* 1987, pp. 240–241, no. 135). Schäfer concluded that the Köln-Braunsfeld cage cup was finished by cutting. Emboldened by this observation, he used cold-working techniques to make an exact replica of the Daruvar cage cup (**88**), which he completed in 1964.

At about the same time, Josef Welzel, an instructor at the State Glass School at Hadamar, Germany, having failed to convince his colleagues that cage cups were finished by cold working, resolved to demonstrate that this is indeed possible. Beginning in the 1960s, Welzel produced a number of wheel-cut replicas of cage cups, including the Köln-Braunsfeld beaker (**90**) and the Lycurgus Cup (**89**) (Welzel 1978). Subsequently, beginning about 1985, the late George D. Scott of Edinburgh, U.K., made replicas and imitations of cage cups, including the hanging lamp in The Corning Museum of Glass (**81**) and the large bowl-shaped vessel from Hohen-Sülzen, Germany (Scott 1991, 1993). Scott also produced a series of four objects illustrating stages of the manner in which he believed the Corning cage cup was produced (**91**), and he wrote a detailed study about the traces of cold working with wheels and files or similar hand-held tools on the Lycurgus Cup (Scott 1995). These replicas, and others, clearly demonstrate that cage cups *can* be produced by a combination of blowing and cold working.

What they do not demonstrate, however, is that Roman cage cups *must* have been made in this manner, and Rosemarie Lierke has argued strenuously that, while Roman cage cups were finished by cold working, the blanks were made in a mold (see, for example, Lierke 1995 and 2001). Briefly stated, Lierke proposes that the blanks were made by using a plunger to press a mass of molten glass into a mold made of plaster or some other suitable material, thereby forming a cup-shaped element that was destined to become the cage. Next, while the glass was still soft, a hollow, perforated mold, exactly the same size and shape as the plunger, was placed inside it. Another mass of molten glass was then pressed into the inner mold, and some of the hot glass was forced through the perforations. The second mass, therefore, formed both the cup and the bridges connecting the inner and outer walls. After annealing, the plaster mold was removed by dissolving it in water, and the cage was produced by cutting, grinding, and polishing. Lierke maintains that several features of ancient cage cups, such as the shapes of some of the bubbles, the presence of bridges that do not reach the cage or show no signs of cold working, and "hot scratches" on the interior of some examples, indicate that the blanks were made by pressing in rotating molds rather than blowing. The debate continues, although it is difficult to imagine how Roman glassworkers

FIGURE 2
The Köln-Braunsfeld cage cup. Roman Empire, first half of the fourth century. H. 12.1 cm, D. (rim) 10.1 cm. Römisch-Germanisches Museum, Cologne (RGM 60.1).

could have used Lierke's method to achieve the precision required to make the outer wall of even thickness, to center the plaster mold in the glass-lined primary mold, and to create a multicolored outer wall comparable with the wall of the Köln-Braunsfeld cage cup. I suspect that they formed the blank by blowing, applied and marvered any additional colors intended to become parts of the cage, and made the cage exclusively by cold-worked mechanical means.

Mosaic Glass

David Whitehouse

MOSAIC GLASS is the name commonly given to objects made from a patchwork of preformed elements placed in a mold and heated until they fuse. These elements were created from canes: composite strips or bars of glass that often show patterns in cross section. The canes were broken into slices or short lengths that were assembled in patterns and fused. The simplest way to fuse the slices was on a plate or similar flat surface, which was inserted into a furnace for heating. The single piece of glass was then placed in or over a mold and reheated until it became soft, and the mold imparted the shape of the finished object. Many scholars prefer the term *mosaic glass* to *millefiori*, except in the case of Venetian or *façon de Venise* glass of Renaissance and early modern Europe.

Ancient Mosaic Glass

The earliest glass canes were made in the Middle East in the second millennium B.C. Excavations at Tell al-Rimah in northern Iraq yielded fragments of a cylindrical beaker made of slices of monochrome black, white, and green canes arranged in a pattern of chevrons. They were found in an archeological context of about 1350–1250 B.C. At a slightly later date (about 1250–1200 B.C.), large numbers of spirally twisted black and white canes were used to decorate the doorway of the ziggurat (stepped temple) at Choga Zanbil in southwestern Iran. At two other sites in Iran, Hasanlu and Marlik, fragments of vessels made with cane slices have been found in deposits of the late second or early first millennium B.C.

In Egypt, beginning in the 18th Dynasty (which lasted from about 1550 to 1292 B.C.), some small vessels made by the technique known as core forming were decorated with spirally twisted canes of two or three colors. Typically, these canes were heated until they became soft, and they were applied to the rim or body of the vessel in a continuous horizontal band.

Despite these precocious uses of canes and cane slices, fused mosaic glass objects do not seem to have been produced in any significant numbers until the Hellenistic period, which began in 323 B.C., following the death of Alexander the Great, and ended with the establishment of the Roman Empire in 31 B.C. In Egypt, the Hellenistic period coincided with the rule of the Ptolemaic dynasty.

Two distinct traditions of virtuoso glassmaking emerged in the Hellenistic world: the production in Egypt, and perhaps elsewhere, of small, often pictorial mosaic glass inlays, and the manufacture in Egypt, and probably elsewhere, of fine tableware. The inlays include both components of composite figures (collars and skirts, for example) and plaques. Many of these objects are minutely detailed and are the result of creating canes with elaborate patterns or pictorial elements in cross section, assembling groups of canes to make the desired image, and then fusing them—a process that might be repeated numerous times until the pattern or picture was complete. This intricate creation was then heated until it became soft and was stretched. As the length increased, the cross section diminished, and the image became miniaturized. The canes were then cut into slices. In some cases, notably a series of theatrical masks, two slices depicting half of the image were assembled side by side to produce a complete picture (**77** and **78**).

Hellenistic mosaic glass vessels are no less remarkable (Grose 1989, pp. 185–197; *Wolf Collection* 1994, pp. 63–71). They form a distinctive component of an entirely new kind of glassware: luxurious services, designed for eating and drinking, that came into use in the late third or early second century B.C. Frequently known as the Canosa Group, after an early find-place in southeastern Italy, these vessels include dishes, bowls, plates, and cups. The majority of the objects in the Canosa Group are almost colorless, while others have gilded and painted decoration, display gold foil sandwiched between two fused layers of glass, or are made of mosaic glass. All of these objects were cast in molds, and, after annealing, they were meticulously finished by grinding and polishing. At their best, they are exquisite.

The mosaic glass objects in the Canosa Group are of two types. The first type consists of vessels composed of cane slices that were arranged in the desired pattern (which may be more or less random), fused to form a single mass, and reheated to permit the mass to slump into or over a former mold that imparted the shape of the finished object. The second type comprises vessels constructed from lengths of colorless and opaque white spirally twisted canes fused to form a single mass that was reheated and formed by slumping. Such objects are sometimes known as "lace" or "network" mosaic glass, or by the Italian term applied to Renaissance canes of this type: *reticello* (literally, a small net).

We know far too little about the Canosa Group—where the objects were made, for example. Nevertheless, they form the first ensembles of glass vessels that may be described as "services": objects made specifically to be used together for elegant meals and drinking parties.

We have one other fixed point in the history of mosaic glass in the Hellenistic period: the glass from a ship that was wrecked off the island of Antikythera about 80 B.C. or a decade or two later. The most remarkable object salvaged from the wreck was a corroded mechanical device for calculating astronomical events, but historians

FIGURE 1
Mosaic glass bowl. Probably eastern Mediterranean, late second–first century B.C. D. 12.4 cm. The Corning Museum of Glass (55.1.2).

of glass were delighted that the divers also recovered examples of fine glassware. This material includes both monochrome and mosaic glass vessels. The mosaic glass objects are small bowls with tall foot-rings. They belong to a variety of mosaic glass not found in the Canosa Group: vessels that include lengths of canes arranged to create a striped effect. These ribbonlike patterns continued to be popular through the decades on either side of the year A.D. 1—the main period of production of mosaic glass in the Roman Empire.

During the reign of the first Roman emperor, Augustus (27 B.C.–A.D. 14), industries from many parts of the Mediterranean relocated to or opened branches in Italy, which was now the undisputed center of political power and wealth.

Glassmaking prospered in Roman Italy. For at least half a century, while glassblowing emerged as the most common technique of forming vessels, traditional methods of shaping objects by slumping preformed disks or disklike masses of glass continued. These traditional methods included the production of mosaic glass, usually to make vessels for eating and drinking: dishes, bowls, and cups.

Most early Roman mosaic glass falls into three large categories, two of which were characteristic of the Canosa Group. The first of these consists of objects made from slices of canes. Individual slices may have star-shaped or spiral patterns, and they frequently form a carpetlike design (Fig. 1). The second category employs *reticello* canes to produce an overall lacelike effect.

FIGURE 2
Ribbon glass cup. Roman Empire, about 25 B.C.–A.D. 50. D. 8.6 cm. The Corning Museum of Glass (72.1.11).

The third category of early Roman mosaic glass was made in the tradition of the striped vessels on the Antikythera wreck. This "ribbon mosaic" glass consists mostly of shallow bowls with decoration divided into quadrants of stripes, arranged in V-shaped patterns, that converge on a single cane slice at the center of the floor (Fig. 2). The ornament is brightly colored: transparent green, yellow, purple, blue, and red, together with opaque white. Many of these stripes are sandwiches of transparent colored glass separated by an opaque white layer. Similar vessels included colorless layers separated by a strip of gold foil. All three categories—vessels made of slices, *reticello* canes, and ribbons of colored glass—were imitated in the 19th century. **69**, for example, is a copy of a ribbon mosaic glass bowl found at Pompeii.

Mosaic Glass in the Renaissance

Glassmaking in Venice blossomed in the mid-15th century, when a dazzling array of new and often luxurious Venetian products was in demand all over Europe. Among the techniques practiced by the Venetian glassmakers of the Renaissance was the manufacture of blown glass vessels decorated with slices of canes. Such objects have no ancient precedents, and they appear to be one of the many innovations in glassmaking developed on the Venetian island of Murano.

The impetus for this millefiori (literally, a thousand flowers) decoration probably came from beadmaking, which was an important aspect of the Venetian glass industry. Multicolored canes were made in large quantities and were used to produce vast numbers of beads, which were exported to many parts of the known world. Perhaps the most popular beads were known as *rosette* (little roses), and they were used to make rosaries. The canes for *rosette* were made by pressing successive gathers of white, red, and bright blue glass into a star-shaped mold. Seen in cross section, the canes had a pattern of concentric star-shaped bands of the three different colors. Short lengths of canes were ground to form roughly egg-shaped beads that displayed the pattern at either end.

In addition to making beads, slices of *rosette* canes were used for two purposes: to create balls and ball-shaped pendants, and to decorate vessels. The ball-shaped objects consist of a cluster of cane slices in a matrix of colorless glass. About 1500, Marcantonio Coccio Sabellico, in the third book of his *Opera Omnia*, titled *De Venetae urbis situ* (On the site of the city of Venice), described the objects thus: "But consider to whom did it first occur to include in a little ball all the sorts of flowers which clothe the meadows in Spring" (*Paperweights* 1978, p. 13).

The millefiori vessels, which were never common, were made by partly inflating a bubble of molten glass and rolling it on assorted cane slices, then making sure the slices were flush with the surface of the bubble, and finally completing the inflation so that the object had the desired shape and size.

The Rediscovery of Roman Mosaic Glass

Roman mosaic glass began to attract serious attention shortly after the discovery of Pompeii in 1748 brought to light antiquities of all kinds (Hollister 1987). Four years later, Anne Claude Philippe Caylus (1692–1765) began to publish his seven-volume *Recueil d'antiquités égyptiennes, étrusques, grecques, romaines, et gauloises* (Collection of Egyptian, Etruscan, Greek, Roman, and Gaulish antiquities). The first volume contains a discussion (on pages 293–310) about how Roman mosaic glass may have been made. Johann Joachim Winckelmann (1717–1768) returned to this question in 1764, and the eminent German chemist Martin Heinrich Klaproth (1743–1817) owned a fragment of blown glass decorated with *rosette* cane slices that he believed to be Roman but was clearly made on Murano. By 1786, a German named Brückmann was reported to be studying the question of how Roman mosaic glass was made, and in his *Nachträge zu meinem Werke*, published in 1827, Johann Heinrich Carl Minutoli (1772–1846) reported that imitations of Roman objects were already being produced in Italy (Minutoli 1827, p. 296).

A group of mosaic glass bowls and dishes in the Antikensammlungen und Glyptothek in Munich represents this late 18th- to early 19th-century production of imitations of Roman originals. The objects bear little resemblance to Roman mosaic glass, Renaissance glass from Murano, or later 19th-century Venetian products. Indeed, they are in a class of their own. The vessels are documented as formerly belonging to Edward Dodwell (1767–1832), an English traveler and antiquarian who lived for a while in Rome, formed a collection of antiquities, and placed it in the Institute for Archeological Correspondence, which was established in Rome in 1828. We may be confident, therefore, that these pieces are unusually early imitations of ancient mosaic glass and that they were made before 1828, when Dodwell donated them to the institute.

Later 19th-Century Mosaic Glass

The focal point of the 19th-century revival of mosaic glass was Murano, and the driving force behind the reintroduction of mosaic glass on Murano was Vincenzo Moretti (1835–1901). Moretti began his career in glassmaking as a lowly *tiracanna* (cane puller) in Pietro Bigaglia's bead factory. While working for Bigaglia, Moretti experimented in his spare time with glass compositions, colors, and compatibility. His proficiency caught the attention of one of the giants of 19th-century Venetian glassmaking: Antonio Salviati, the founder (in 1872) of The Venice and Murano Glass Company. When, in 1867, Salviati opened a factory for the manufacture of colored glass for mosaics, he hired Moretti. Two years later, Moretti and his colleague Luigi Dalla Venezia won for Salviati, at the Second Exhibition of Murano Glass, a gold medal for their imitations of semiprecious stones and their creation of numerous other colors. In fact, Salviati offered no fewer than 2,700 different shades!

Salviati was a strong proponent of teaching his employees the elements of design. In this, he followed the example of Abbot Vincenzo Zanetti, who, in 1861, had assembled the core collection of the Museo Vetrario on Murano, the purpose of which was to inspire Muranese glassworkers to emulate and perhaps outshine the masters of earlier generations.

Thanks to the activities of Zanetti, Moretti was well prepared for a field trip in 1871, when Salviati took some of his glassworkers to the mainland city of Brescia, 100 miles from Murano, to study glass objects preserved in the museum there. The workers were particularly impressed by a Roman mosaic glass bowl that they resolved to imitate. At about the same time, Salviati returned from a business trip to Rome with a collection of recently discovered fragments of ancient mosaic glass.

Vincenzo Moretti was the key to establishing Salviati as Murano's leading maker of mosaic glass. He designed canes with intricate patterns (most of which bear little resemblance to ancient canes), and he made mosaic glass vessels that are disconcertingly similar to Hellenistic and Roman originals (**69**, **71**, and **72**). They were known by the name *millefiori*, a term that had been coined in the 15th century. However, Moretti's designs are most often associated, not with Salviati, but with The Venice and Murano Glass Company, the name that Salviati gave to his business in 1872.

Alessandro Castellani, a prominent Rome-based jeweler and collector of antiquities, was another important figure in the rebirth of ancient glass on 19th-century Murano.

In 1873, Castellani donated examples of ancient mosaic glass to the Museo Vetrario. Zanetti hailed the Castellani gift as models for modern versions of ancient glass. The museum received a second donation of ancient glass in 1876, when Alexander Nesbitt presented Zanetti with 36 examples of early glassmaking.

Moretti, therefore, had a rich harvest of objects to copy. These objects taught him and his colleagues that Hellenistic and Roman glassworkers (they thought of them as Etruscans) had produced mosaic glass by making canes with patterns visible in cross section, arranging slices of these canes to form disks, fusing the disks, and reheating them so that they could be formed in or over molds. At the end of this process, the vessels were cut and polished to produce a uniform, shiny surface.

Moretti's results were spectacular. First shown at the 1878 world's fair in Paris, they were acclaimed as the "loveliest gem of Italian industrial art . . . the only major innovations in the glassmaking field" (**61**). Zanetti now abandoned the word *millefiori* and introduced the term *vetri murrini*, which had been used by the ancient Roman encyclopedist Pliny the Elder to refer to some kind of precious and exotic vessel—perhaps (as Zanetti believed) mosaic glass.

It is hardly surprising that, after its enthusiastic reception in 1878, Moretti's mosaic glass enjoyed considerable success. Indeed, it became one of the signature products of The Venice and Murano Glass Company. Moretti faithfully imitated ancient glasses in the Louvre, the Museo Archeologico Nazionale in Naples (**69**), and the Museum of Art and Industry in Vienna. Moretti and his co-workers examined ancient originals, and on the basis of their firsthand research, they made their modern replicas. Moretti himself identified his creations by including a cane slice containing the monogram "VM" (Vincenzo Moretti; **62** and **71**). Without the giveaway signature, it would be difficult to distinguish visually between the most subtle of Moretti's imitations and Hellenistic or Roman originals.

In 1900, Moretti left The Venice and Murano Glass Company to join his sons in establishing a new company, Luigi Moretti [Vincenzo's son] and Company. Luigi, who had worked with his father at The Venice and Murano Glass Company, began to make mosaic glass portrait canes in 1888, including images of his father, Kings Victor Emmanuel II and Umberto I, the Italian general Giuseppe Garibaldi, and Kaiser Wilhelm I, all of whom (and others) appear on a plaque made in or after 1894.

At about the same time, Giovanni Barovier (1839–1908), who, with his brothers, worked for Salviati, produced numerous *murrine* (as slices of complex canes were known in and after the 19th century), often based on Roman originals. Barovier made careful drawings of ancient mosaic glass (**76**), then produced variations on their designs and incorporated them into vessels (**70**). As with the portrait canes of Giacomo Franchini and Luigi Moretti, and with much late 19th-century cameo glass (see pages 14–17), these objects would never be confused with ancient originals, but their ultimate source of inspiration is obvious.

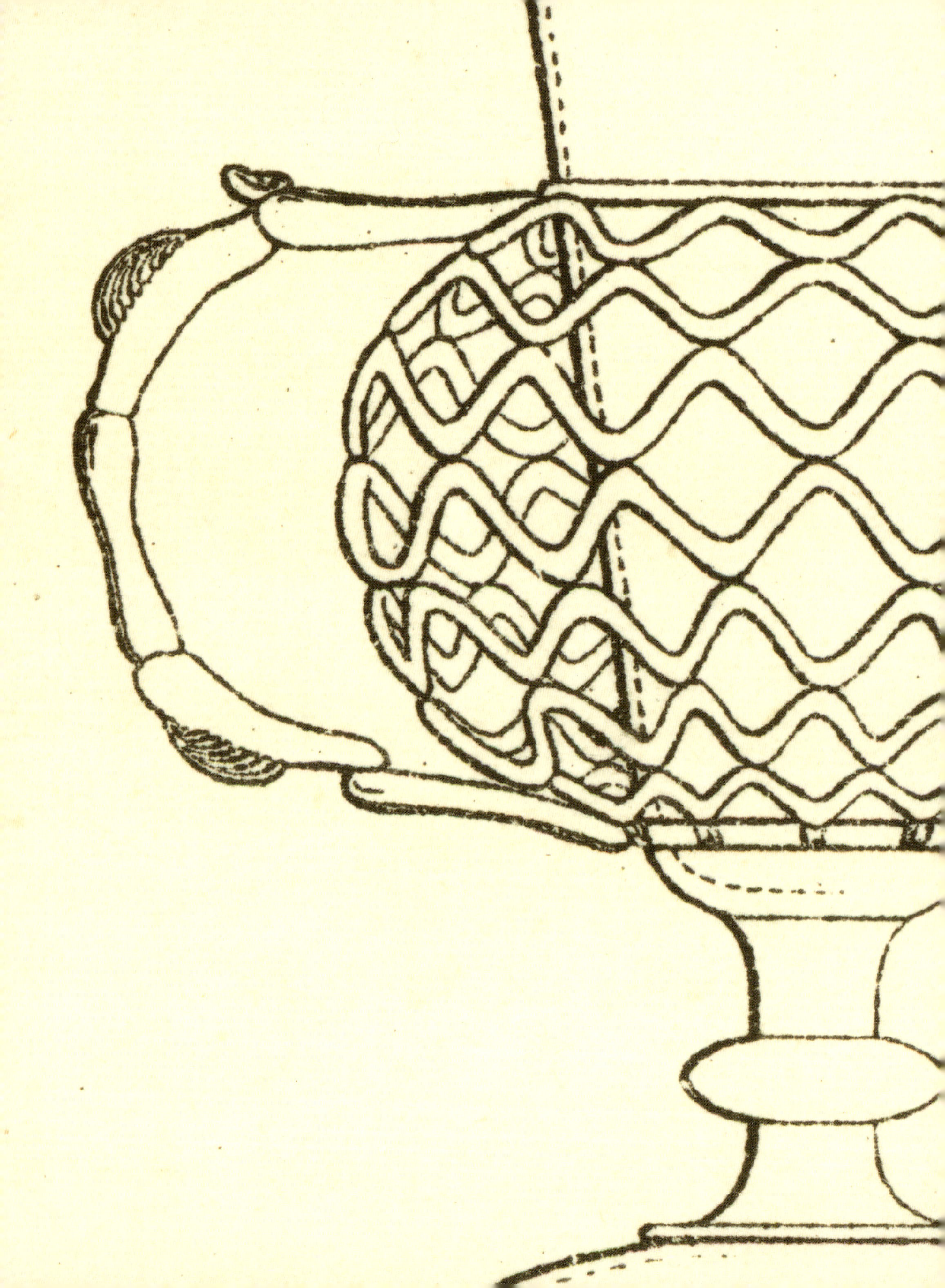

Ehrenfeld and Felmer Imitations of Roman Glass Vessels

Dunja Zobel-Klein and Michael J. Klein

During the late 19th century, many Roman glass vessels were excavated in cities along the Rhine. Most of these objects were undamaged because they had been placed in stone sarcophagi, and they were highly valued for their delicacy and elegance. They also inspired glassmakers to produce imitations. Two of the leading European producers or dealers of these imitations were the Ehrenfeld glassworks near Cologne and the Felmer glassware business in Mainz. Their reproductions of Roman glass vessels were recently presented in two exhibitions at the Landesmuseum Mainz. Publications include research on the Ehrenfeld glassworks (Zobel-Klein 2003b) and the Felmer glass trade (Ricke 1999; Zobel-Klein 2006b), as well as discussions of the sketchbooks of Oskar Rauter (director of the Ehrenfeld glassworks; Zobel-Klein 2003a) and his business relations throughout Europe (*idem* 2005). A study of the Ehrenfeld catalogs and supplements is in preparation (*idem* forthcoming).

Ehrenfeld

The Catalogs of Roman Imitations

In addition to introducing a department of decorative arts at the glasshouse in Ehrenfeld, Oskar Rauter (1840–1913) set the guidelines for the making of imitations of Roman glass there (Fig. 1). Between 1881 and 1893, he published two catalogs and two supplements illustrating the range of Roman reproductions created by his firm

Acknowledgments. We thank our colleagues in museums and archives for the assistance they provided.

FIGURE 1
Salesroom in Ehrenfeld glassworks, 1892.

(Schäfke 1979; Zobel-Klein 2003b). They include drawings of the vessels and brief descriptions of their names, colors, dimensions, and decorative features. All of these objects were numbered, which permits them to be precisely identified.

Rauter's first catalog, issued in October 1881, presented 16 imitations of Roman glass, including six jugs, four beakers, and one set. Each vessel was marked with a small circular paper label showing the Ehrenfeld trademark: a *Römer* inscribed "EHRENFELD." Because the paper labels adhered poorly, the trademark was etched on the bottom of each object by the time the second catalog was published in February 1886 (**109**). That catalog contained all of the vessels from the 1881 catalog and introduced 14 new reproductions, considerably expanding the range of shapes and decorations. Some of these "Roman" objects were grouped as wine and water sets. A jug and one of the water sets were offered in two colors.

In the first supplement, which appeared in November 1888, only one Roman imitation was included: a water set. The second supplement, published in January 1893, presented two beakers and a drinking horn.

The catalogs and supplements contain a total of 36 imitations of Roman glasses.

As Rauter explained in a letter of May 1886, the number of Roman reproductions in the second catalog was restricted for financial reasons. He also noted that while the study of Roman glassmaking techniques had been very instructive, sales figures were not as high as he had anticipated (Zobel-Klein 2003b, p. 179).

In addition to noting the museums and private collections in which the Roman originals of his imitations were housed, Rauter provided names for some of his glasses that offer intriguing insights for researchers. For example, the jug "Drusus" was inspired by a large monument in Mainz honoring the Roman general Drusus the Elder (d. 9 B.C.). Rauter studied the Roman model for this vessel in the Mainz museum.

The "Agrippina" water set was named for Agrippina the Younger (d. A.D. 59), wife of the Roman emperor Claudius. She was born in Oppidum Ubiorum, which was later named Colonia Agrippinensis after her; that name, in turn, was adapted for the present-day city of Cologne. Roman colorless glass jugs and beakers with blue, opaque yellow, and opaque white snake-thread decoration are very common in the Cologne region (**103**), and Rauter studied several examples in the Cologne museum. One of these types of vessels was the prototype for a small flask named "Colonia" (**110**). It was excavated in Cologne and accessioned by the Bonn museum (Fig. 2).

FIGURE 2
Roman imitations produced in Ehrenfeld glassworks, late 19th century. "Colonia" flask (23.397) is decorated with blue and white trails. H. (tallest) 33 cm. Römisch-Germanisches Museum, Cologne (left to right: *23.399, 23.398, 23.397, 23.395, zu N 50, 23.394*).

FIGURE 3
Roman jug in the Charvet Collection that served as the model for the "Claudia" jug made by Ehrenfeld glassworks.

Rauter noted that the Roman originals for his imitations were housed in museums in Bonn, London, Trier, Cologne (**102**, **104**, and **105**), Berlin, Nuremberg, and Amsterdam; in the Aus'm Weerth, Disch (**47**), and Merkens Collections; and in the collection of the Bonn Society of Antiquarians. This listing underscores the extensive journeys

FIGURE 4
Two-handled flask, sold as a flower vase. Germany, Ehrenfeld glassworks, late 19th century. H. 20.5 cm. Grassi-Museum, Leipzig (V 5534).

that Rauter made in seeking inspiration for his imitations of Roman glasses, which are also reflected in his sketchbooks containing many hundreds of drawings of Roman glass vessels.

Rauter also studied such richly illustrated books as the catalog of the Charvet Collection (Froehner 1879). He took a plate from this publication (Fig. 3) as the model for his "Claudia" jug. Several drawings from the magnificent plates in the catalog of the Slade Collection (*Slade Collection* 1871) were added to his sketchbooks.

Ehrenfeld's Roman Imitations

The production of Roman-inspired glasses at Ehrenfeld included a wide range of jugs and beakers: a jug within a jug (**111**), beakers with six or nine indentations, a water set consisting of a pot with eight indentations and two beakers with six indentations, various kinds of bowls, a two-handled flask serving as a flower vase (Fig. 4), several sets, a fish (**112**), and a drinking horn.

FIGURE 5
Jug with oblique trails. Germany, Ehrenfeld glassworks, late 19th century. H. 31.7 cm. Museum im Andreasstift, Worms.

Rauter indicated that most of the decoration on these objects was formed by winding hot trails of glass around the body (Fig. 5) or by applying blobs and trails, or snake-thread trails. The jugs and pots had various sorts of handles; two-ribbed handles were rather frequently employed. Only one vessel, a small bowl, was ornamented with facet cutting.

Chain-Handled Jugs. Rauter was especially interested in handles, including ribbon handles, rod handles, and ornamental chain handles. As can be seen in his sketchbooks, he studied pitchers with chain handles in several museums (Zobel-Klein 2003a, pp. 172–174). He was particularly enthusiastic about the conical jug with a chain handle in the Charvet Collection (Froehner 1879, pl. XIX; Zobel-Klein 2005, p. 44), now in The Metropolitan Museum of Art, New York, and in his sketchbook he copied the large color plate (Fig. 6) from the catalog of that collection. He also added to his production a chain-handled jug based on a Roman original in the Bonn museum. This ovoid, ribbed object features a trailed rim and foot-ring. Jugs with chain handles are often biconical or ovoid, and sometimes globular, but there are other shapes as well (Zobel-Klein 2006a). The largest collection of chain-handled jugs, consisting of about 20 examples, is in the Landesmuseum Mainz (*idem* 1999).

FIGURE 6
Roman chain-handled jug in the Charvet Collection, which was studied and sketched by Oskar Rauter.

Late Roman Glass with Snake-Thread Decoration. This small group of imitations consists of two bowls, a cantharus based on an original in the Bonn museum, and a conical beaker after a model in the Nuremberg museum. These four vessels were made of yellowish green glass decorated with shiny black blobs, festoons, zigzag trails, snake-thread decoration, and lattice patterns.

FIGURE 7
"Agricola" jug. Germany, Ehrenfeld glassworks, late 19th century. H. 16.5 cm. Museum Wiesbaden (13827).

The quality and appearance of the glass are remarkable. The four originals were made late in the Roman era, when glass was full of tiny bubbles, dark specks, and streaks. The Ehrenfeld imitations, however, are made of glass without any impurities. Rauter also changed the colors of the ornamentation, especially with his imitation of the Bonn cantharus. He inserted a drawing of this vessel in his sketchbook, and he provided a detailed description of the blue and brown hues of the blobs and zigzag trails.

Rauter's sketchbook indicates that he studied the prototypes of the two bowls when they were displayed as recently excavated pieces at the "Exposition rétrospective de l'art industriel" in Brussels in 1880 (Zobel-Klein 2005, pp. 42–43). The originals are now housed in the Musée Archéologique de Namur. While Rauter's sketches represent the shapes of the Roman bowls exactly, he varied the decoration by adding blobs to the festoons and by changing the color from brown to black.

Rauter also studied incomplete vessels such as a conical beaker with lattice-shaped decoration (*idem* 2003a, pp. 170–172). More than a third of this object had been lost when Rauter made a drawing of it in his sketchbook. Although its trails are brown, Rauter described them as opaque black because of their thickness—and he deliberately changed the color in fashioning his imitation.

As is indicated in Rauter's various writings, another of his concerns was the dating of late Roman glass. Some of the late Roman bowls and beakers with trailed and blobbed decoration are housed in the Mainz museum (Klein 1999). While some of these vessels came from early Frankish graves, Rauter was able to identify them as late Roman (Zobel-Klein 2003a, pp. 168–171). He also studied and drew late Roman beakers with trailed decoration in museums in Berlin and Wiesbaden.

The "Agricola" Jug. One of Rauter's favorite objects was a small jug in The British Museum that had formerly been part of the Slade Collection (*idem* 2005, pp. 43–44). The body is of blue glass with white trails combed upward into festoons, and there are some green spiral trails on the lip and neck; the handle is green as well. Rauter made two imitations of the jug, one in blue and the other in green (Fig. 7; *idem* 2003b, pp. 188–189), each of which was decorated with combed white festoons.

Wine and Water Sets. In his catalogs, Rauter offered sets consisting of a jug and two or three beakers: an "Agrippina" water set, a "Plinius" wine set, a "Livia" water set, and a "Roman" water set (*ibid.*, pp. 185–186). The decoration of three of these sets is unique in the Ehrenfeld production of Roman imitations.

Rauter studied the models for the "Plinius" and "Agrippina" sets, as well as other Roman vessels, in the Bonn museum. The bottle and each of the three beakers of the "Plinius" set are covered with 72 and 24 pincered projections respectively. In his catalog, Rauter described this decoration as little pearls or beads.

FIGURE 8
Roman jug in the Slade Collection that served as the model for a jug in the "Livia" water set made by Ehrenfeld glassworks.

The jug and the three beakers of the "Agrippina" set were offered in two colors: yellowish green vessels with opaque yellow trails, and vessels and decoration in *Meergrün* (sea green). Both versions varied the color of the Roman originals.

The prototypes of the vessels in the "Livia" set came from different collections. Rauter sketched the jug with a trefoil-shaped mouth, formerly in the Slade Collection and now in The British Museum, from the catalog by Alexander Nesbitt (Fig. 8; *Slade Collection* 1871, fig. 56), and he studied the conical beaker with festoon decoration in Cologne, where it was part of the famous Disch Collection. In his imitations of these vessels, Rauter added the festoons from the beaker to the jug (Fig. 9), creating a unity of design for the set.

Cage Cups. Because of limited sales expectations, Rauter was required to restrict the number of his Roman imitations. As a result, some of the most interesting ancient vessels, such as the cage cups that he studied on numerous occasions (Zobel-Klein 2003a, pp. 159–166), were never part of the Ehrenfeld production. Nevertheless, his drawings and other documentation of these objects have proved to be extremely valuable.

In 1844, two cage cups were excavated in Cologne (see page 27). These extraordinary vessels were acquired by museums in Berlin and Munich. Rauter studied the Berlin example in 1882, making a drawing (**83**) and taking notes on the technology and design of the object. The construction of the meshes was particularly interesting to him, so he created a separate drawing of the base and described it in detail. Another very important cage cup was excavated in Hohen-Sülzen in 1869. With its hemispherical bowl measuring 21 centimeters in diameter, it is the largest cage cup known, but it was found in fragments. Rauter drew five images of the cage cup in his sketchbook. Decades later, the object was restored. However, during World War II, one of the cage cups from Cologne (displayed in Berlin) and the Hohen-Sülzen cup were lost, so Rauter's drawings are a primary source of information about them. Rauter also drew a fragment of a cage cup in The British Museum.

FIGURE 9
Roman imitations produced by Ehrenfeld glassworks, late 19th century. Jug from "Livia" water set is large vessel at right. H. (tallest) 26.8 cm. Landesgewerbeanstalt, Nuremberg, housed in the Germanisches Nationalmuseum, Nuremberg (front to back: *LGA 7083, LGA 6352, LGA 6242/1, LGA 6238, LGA 6240, LGA 11357).*

Felmer

Ten years after Oskar Rauter began to make Roman glass imitations in Ehrenfeld, Bernhard Ludwig Felmer II started to sell such imitations in Mainz. In his first catalog, dated May 1890, Felmer offered 64 copies, nearly twice the quantity of the entire Ehrenfeld production. Between 1890 and 1900, Felmer expanded his output to an astonishing 117 copies of Roman originals (Ricke 1999, pp. 144–147; Zobel-Klein 2006b, pp. 148–156).

FIGURE 10
Former property of Felmer glassware business (two buildings at right) near Mainz Cathedral, shown in 1952 photograph.

Felmer (1838–1906) came from a large family of glaziers (Zobel-Klein 2006b, pp. 137–145). His grandfather, Anton Felmer (1766–1828), had settled in Mainz and worked there toward the end of the 18th century. His three sons also worked as glaziers. One of them, Ludwig (1802–1865), expanded the family's activities and registered a glassware business and store in 1829. In late 1830 or early 1831, the business was relocated to a piece of property near Mainz Cathedral (Fig. 10). As an inventory of his personal property and real estate indicates, Ludwig was very successful, expanding his firm to include porcelain as well as glass. When he died, his widow initially took control of the business, but in 1867 it was sold at auction to his eldest son, Bernhard Ludwig. Unlike his father, Bernhard Ludwig did not work as a glazier, but only as a businessman.

When large quantities of well-preserved glass vessels were excavated in Roman cemeteries in Mainz during the last quarter of the 19th century, Felmer proceeded to have copies of them made. He displayed these copies at the 1893 world's fair in Chicago and at the Paris exposition in 1900. Just two years later, however, he closed his firm and retired.

Catalogs of Roman Imitations

In addition to his 1890 catalog, Felmer published two undated supplements, both of which note that his glass won awards at the Chicago world's fair. So the supplements must have been issued between 1893 and 1900, when Felmer received another prize at the Paris exposition (Ricke 1999, pp. 148–149; Zobel-Klein 2006b, p. 156).

The introduction to the catalog states that all of Felmer's imitations were based on Roman originals in the Mainz museum (Zobel-Klein 2006b, pp. 145–148). The first supplement introduced 12 new types of Roman-inspired vessels to augment the original 64 designs, as well as some Frankish and medieval German imitations, again after prototypes in the Mainz museum. Only Roman copies are included in the second supplement (Ricke 1999, pp. 144–147). In the catalog, the vessels are illustrated by photographs (Fig. 11), and their colors, handles, and decoration are sometimes briefly

FIGURE 11
Glass shown in Felmer catalog, May 1890.

described. In some cases, Roman numerals are added to the production number, which indicates that copies were offered in two or more sizes, intentionally varying the sizes and proportions of the Roman originals.

Imitations of Roman Glass Vessels

Felmer's catalog introduction also states that his imitations of Roman vessels were manufactured in one of Germany's leading glassworks. Although the name of this firm is not provided, it was probably the Josephinenhütte in Silesia. There are three interesting aspects of Felmer's imitations. First, they are of very high quality, as is suggested by the awards they received at the world's fairs of 1893 and 1900. The surface of these vessels is intentionally iridescent, which was regarded as an important sign of technical progress in glassmaking. Second, they are important documents of lost Roman glass vessels from the Mainz museum (Fig. 12; Klein and Zobel-Klein 2005). Finally, they

FIGURE 12
Felmer copies of Roman originals that are now lost. H. (tallest) 32.8 cm. Römisch-Germanisches Zentralmuseum, Mainz (front, left to right: *18156a, 18147d, 18130a, 18140b*; back, left to right: *18140a, 18134b, 18134a, 18139, 18131*).

FIGURE 13
Jug with flattened body. Roman original (D. 18 cm; right*) is in Landesmuseum Mainz (R 4455); Felmer copy is in Römisch-Germanisches Zentralmuseum, Mainz (18134d).*

had a unique impact on Silesian glassmaking of the early 20th century (Ricke 1999, pp. 151 and 153).

A detailed comparison reveals many differences between Felmer's imitations and their Roman prototypes (Zobel-Klein 2006b, pp. 148–156). For example, the shape and color of a dark green jug with a flattened body were imitated, but the shade of green is lighter and the glass itself is transparent (Fig. 13). The handle of the original was already lost when the vessel was listed with a drawing in the museum's inventory.

One rare type of bowl that fascinated both Rauter and Felmer featured snake-thread trails (Klein and Zobel-Klein 2005, pp. 4–6). It had a large rim, and a drawing and description in one of Rauter's sketchbooks indicates that the vessel and trails were made of colorless glass. This bowl, which was formerly in the Mainz museum, is known from a drawing in the museum's inventory and from a photograph in the Felmer catalog that was first published in 2006 (Zobel-Klein 2006b, p. 147). Felmer offered his imitation of this bowl in two sizes (Fig. 14). Two comparable Roman pieces were recently excavated in France (Cabart 2004, p. 13; *idem* 2005, p. 21).

Another Roman vessel, which was lost during World War II (Klein and Zobel-Klein 2005, pp. 8–10), is unique because of its second handle. The tall cylindrical neck and the large handle, which extends down the wall in a notched trail, are characteris-

FIGURE 14
Felmer copy of bowl with snake-thread trails. H. 5.7 cm, D. 15.8 cm. Römisch-Germanisches Zentralmuseum, Mainz (18156a).

tic features of this type of pitcher, but the eyelet-shaped handle on the opposite side, which is also in the form of a notched trail, marks this jug as outstanding. A drawing and a photograph of the Roman original are found in the museum's inventory and Felmer's catalog respectively (Zobel-Klein 2006b, p. 147). Two imitations of this Roman vessel are known (Fig. 15). Their slight differences are seen in the elaboration of the neck, for example.

A small hemispherical beaker decorated with facet cutting is another of Felmer's imitations, but its facets are ovoid, not circular. Unlike the Roman original, the surface of the imitation is iridescent and frosted, and the facet-cut areas are smooth and polished (Fig. 16).

Felmer's imitation of a Roman beaker is very important because it preserves an inscription in gilded letters that has been rubbed off and is almost illegible on the original. The Latin inscription, written in two lines, reads "VITAM TIBI QUIA SCIS QUID SIT BONUM" (Life to you because you know what is good). The

FIGURE 15
Felmer copy of conical jug with tall neck. H. 24.5 cm. Römisch-Germanisches Zentralmuseum, Mainz (18134a).

FIGURE 16
Facet-cut hemispherical beaker. Roman original (H. 4.2 cm; right) is in Landesmuseum Mainz (R 812); Felmer copy is in Römisch-Germanisches Zentralmuseum, Mainz (18153a).

FIGURE 17
Beaker with Latin inscription in gilded letters. Roman original (H. 11.2 cm; right) is in Landesmuseum Mainz (R 1066); Felmer copy is in Römisch-Germanisches Zentralmuseum, Mainz (18149).

original vessel is almost intact, but it is in very bad condition, so the imitation provides an impression of the Roman object's appearance (Fig. 17).

It is very instructive to compare imitations of Roman vessels sold by Felmer and vessels produced in the Ehrenfeld glassworks. The latter were made with the utmost craftsmanship. The vessels are lightweight and thin-walled, made of very pure transparent glass, and the surface is not iridescent. The overall impression made by the Ehrenfeld vessels is that they are of the highest quality—a quality even greater than that of their Roman models. Although the Felmer copies were produced in one of the leading glassworks, they are heavy and plump rather than delicate. Like their Ehrenfeld counterparts, they are made of glass without impurities. Here, however, the surface is intentionally iridescent, and the vessels have a velvetlike feel.

The Silesian glassworks that made Felmer's copies employed a wide range of decorating techniques. Several types of vessels sold by Felmer were cut in different ways, and none of the ornaments was used more than once.

Felmer's reproductions exerted a considerable influence on Silesian glass vessels. Even when orders from Felmer ceased, production of Roman imitations at the Silesian Josephinenhütte continued. The classical Roman forms were esteemed by Fritz Heckert, one of the prominent artists and designers of Silesian Art Nouveau glass. Imitations made by the Ehrenfeld glasshouse, products of traditional craftsmanship based on detailed studies of Roman originals, are much appreciated because of their excellent quality. But Oskar Rauter's drawings and descriptions of Roman glass vessels are even more valuable because important objects are now lost, and his observations are among the very limited documentation pertaining to them. In addition, his studies of these vessels led to new considerations of their dating, technology, and design. Finally, with his own knowledge of glassmaking, Rauter intended to re-establish ancient Roman craftsmanship, and this resulted in the reproductions that were made in his Ehrenfeld glassworks.

The Making of Roman and 19th-Century Cameo Glass

William Gudenrath

FASCINATION WITH THE PORTLAND VASE—the most celebrated of all ancient Roman glass objects, which has been on display in The British Museum, London, since 1810—intensified in mid-19th-century England. It peaked among Stourbridge glassworkers when the glasshouse owner Benjamin Richardson (1802–1887) announced a competition to reproduce the vase. The prize was to be £1,000. This competition inspired John Northwood (1836–1902) to create his prize-winning copy (**33**) in 1876. As a result, cameo glass instantly became fashionable and was in great demand, and the English cameo glass revival began in earnest (*Cameo Glass* 1982, pp. 42–57; Whitehouse 1994, pp. 17–29).

Since that time, questions about how these exceedingly beautiful objects were made have inspired debate among scholars, collectors, and the curious. Determining how the blanks were made during the Roman period has been a particularly problematic area of research. New observations and investigations comparing cameo glass of the Roman and modern eras may shed light on aspects of this question.

In antiquity, lapidaries who normally cut and engraved hard stones probably also decorated glass blanks, using both rotating soft-stone wheels and sharp hand tools. Written accounts of the late 19th century indicate the employment of essentially the same processes, with the additional aid of hydrofluoric acid, which was used to remove large portions of the overlay before the detail-work began. This modern convenience must have saved enormous amounts of time and labor.

More controversial is the question of how cameo glass blanks were made in antiquity. It has been assumed that, with few exceptions, blanks for Roman cameo glass vessels were produced by glassblowing (Gudenrath and Whitehouse 1990). While some scholars may disagree, the reasons for glassblowing remain convincing, and the arguments against casting, core forming, slumping, or some otherwise unknown combination of these techniques remain strong.[1] Fortunately, the hot-working processes of the 19th century are well understood because of descriptions written during that period.

In the cameo glass working of both ancient and modern times, the outer layer of a blank—usually an intensely opaque white glass—normally had to be of substantial thickness: at least three to four millimeters. This allowed the workers who created the decoration to achieve some of the bolder sculptural effects that we see in the finest objects. These effects include the fairly high relief of some of the figures on the Portland Vase (Fig. 1) and the undercutting that helps to make the vines on the Auldjo Jug (**28**) so vivid (Fig. 2).

Some of the subtle shading effects, as in the delicate wings of the putto on the Portland Vase, required that the point at which the two glasses met be perfectly smooth. This was explored with conspicuous virtuosity by 19th-century English cameo glass craftsmen. For example, the surf and cloud effects of the *Aphrodite* plaque by George Woodall (1892) must have been accomplished by removing opaque white glass bit by tiny bit (Fig. 3). Any substantial bubbles trapped between the two layers of glass in areas where such precision work was intended would have spelled certain disaster.

Close inspection of many ancient cameo glass objects, both complete examples and fragments, in numerous collections (including The Corning Museum of Glass; The British Museum, London [**27** and **28**]; The J. Paul Getty Museum, Malibu [**29** and **30**]; and the Museo Archeologico Nazionale, Naples) reveals that these unattractive bubbles are commonplace. In sharp contrast, a careful examination of 19th-century (and later) cameo glass objects in The Corning Museum of Glass, the Victoria and Albert Museum (London), and the MSC Forsyth Center Galleries at Texas A&M University (College Station) shows an almost total absence of such bubbles. This consistent difference suggests that two completely different manufacturing methods were used to make the blanks for these two distinct groups of objects.

Thanks to thorough documentation, we can be certain of the manner in which at least some cameo glass blanks were made in 19th-century England. In his 1849 book *Curiosities of Glass Making* (**31**), Apsley Pellatt described and illustrated the process of creating "cased glass" (Pellatt 1849, pp. 114–115). By means of glassblowing, a cup "somewhat like the bowl of a wine-glass, or the broad-end of a large egg-shell" was made of colored glass. After the very hot cup was placed in a stand to hold it upright, the glassblower immediately lowered into it a parison of molten colorless glass, then inflated the parison to fill the cup. The glass was reheated, and the usual glassblowing processes could then be used to create a finished article.

1. These arguments will be discussed in Gudenrath and others forthcoming.

FIGURE 1
Detail of the Portland Vase, showing the somewhat high relief cutting.

FIGURE 2
Detail of the Auldjo Jug, showing an area of undercutting.

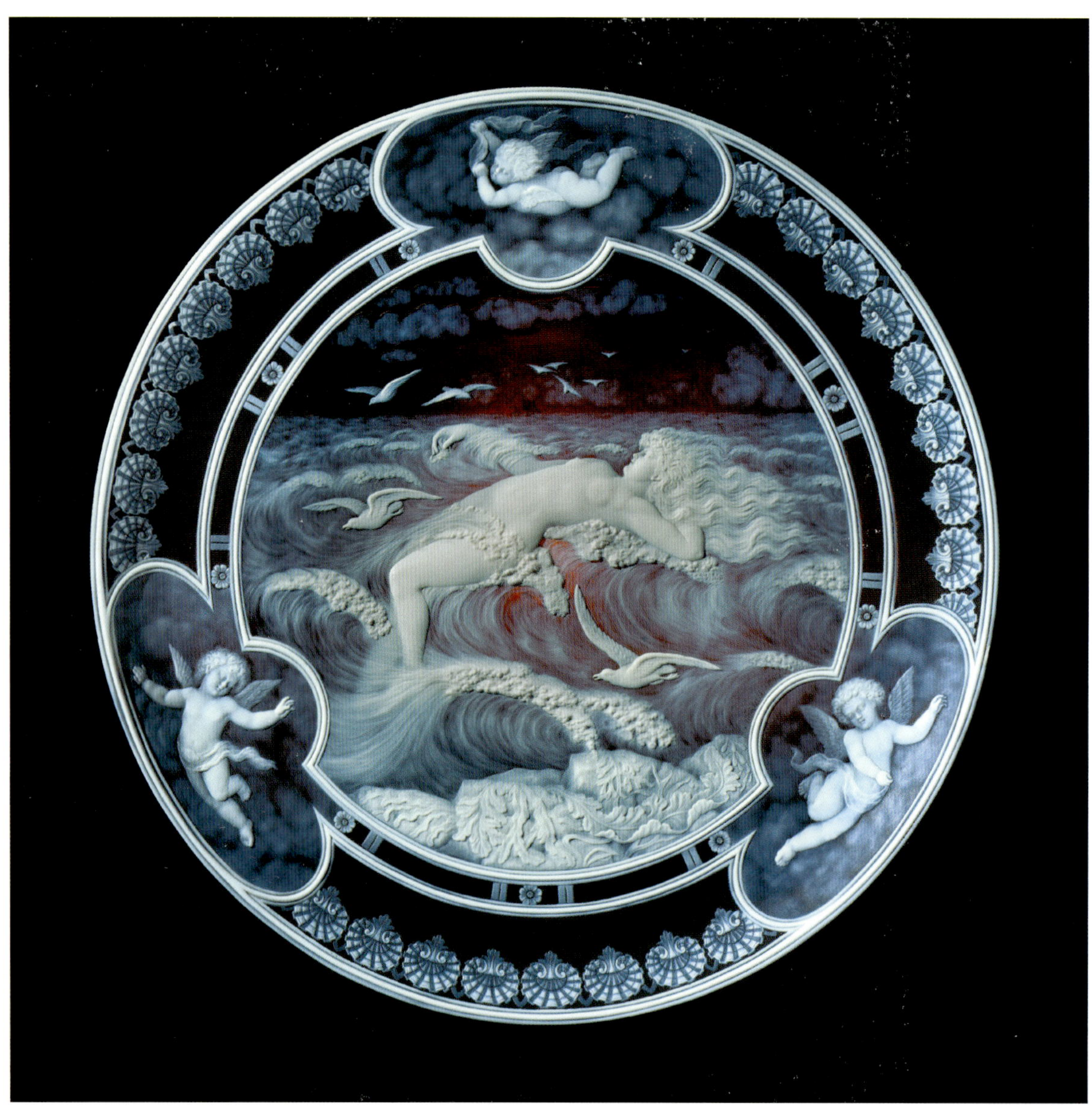

FIGURE 3
Aphrodite *plaque. England, Amblecote, Thomas Webb & Sons, carved by George Woodall, 1892 (signed and dated). D. 33.3 cm. The Corning Museum of Glass (89.2.16, gift of Juliette K. Rakow in memory of Dr. Leonard S. Rakow).*

Apsley Pellatt wrote with exceptional authority. He owned a working glasshouse and was thus intimately familiar with the practicalities of glassworking. In addition, as is evident from his book, he was deeply aware of and presumably knowledgeable about historical glass objects of many periods. The vignette on the title page illustrates the Portland Vase, the Auldjo Jug, and the Blue (or Naples) Vase, the latter two of which had been excavated at Pompeii in the 1830s (**31**). Today these objects remain the iconic examples of ancient cameo glasses that have survived more or less intact. Pellatt stated that the process he illustrated involving an opaque white glass cup was used in the Roman period for making cameo blanks: "The principle of casing . . . was well known to the ancients who made the Portland and Naples Vases" (*ibid.*).

Almost a hundred years later, in 1948, John Northwood II published an account of the effort by his father and a colleague, Philip Pargeter, to create the Northwood replica of the Portland Vase (**33**) in Wordsley, England, between 1873 and 1876. In an earlier publication, he had very thoroughly described a process of creating an overlay "cupping" that is no different from the process reported by Pellatt (Northwood 1924, p. 88). But Northwood also discussed "gathering," a technique with which the worker collects the overlay glass on top of the first layer of glass. Northwood suggested that this was the method used by "the ancients," and he even speculated that the pot containing the opaque white glass was not sufficiently deep to fully accommodate the blue parison, noting that, at their upper attachment points, the handles of the Portland Vase sit squarely atop bare blue glass (see pages 122–129). We can now determine with some certainty which of these two methods was employed in antiquity.

The fundamental problem is that the "cup-overlay method"[2] is a highly refined, technically very difficult procedure that usually requires at least two highly skilled glassblowers, whereas the first ancient cameo glass objects were made in the late first century B.C., not long after the dawn of glassblowing. These two facts seem—and probably are—incompatible. It is difficult enough to accept the great probability that the most famous of all ancient glass objects, the Portland Vase, both dates from as early as 30–20 B.C. and was made by workers utilizing the then little-known process of glassblowing (Painter and Whitehouse 1990c). To argue that the vase was made using such a sophisticated, fully developed refinement of the glassblowing process is therefore incredible.

The much simpler and vastly easier process described by Northwood as "gathering" can be used to achieve nearly the same effect: a thick overlay of one glass atop a layer

2. The terms "cup-overlay method" and "dip-overlay method" were used in the glossary of Tait 1991, pp. 242–244, to help clarify the processes associated with the problematic terms "casing," "flashing," and "overlaying."

FIGURE 4
An elongated parison of blue glass is ready to be dipped in a crucible of opaque white glass.

FIGURE 5
While the glassmaker slowly turns the blowpipe, the blue tube is partly submerged in opaque white glass.

FIGURE 6
After the blowpipe is withdrawn from the opaque white glass, it is held horizontally.

FIGURE 7
The overlay is lightly marvered to ensure that it is perfectly round and concentric with the blue glass.

FIGURE 8
The glasses are briefly reheated and then inflated, beginning the process of forming the body of the vessel.

of contrasting color (Figs. 4–8). The "dip-overlay method" involves nothing more complicated than having the glassblower make a gather of one color of glass on the end of a blowpipe and then dip it into a crucible of molten glass of a different color. This unfailingly leaves a rather thick overlay, just as is seen on ancient cameo glass objects.

Unfortunately, unless it is very carefully executed, the dip-overlay method is likely to trap bubbles at the interface where the two glasses meet (Fig. 9). While the soft glass is being marvered (rolled back and forth on a flat stone or metal surface) in order to give it the required tubular shape, the surface of the glass becomes slightly roughened. If the hardened tube is then dipped, however slowly, into the molten glass that is intended to produce the overlay, the viscous material will fail to flow into the deepest recesses of the uneven surface and leave voids that become unsightly bubbles.

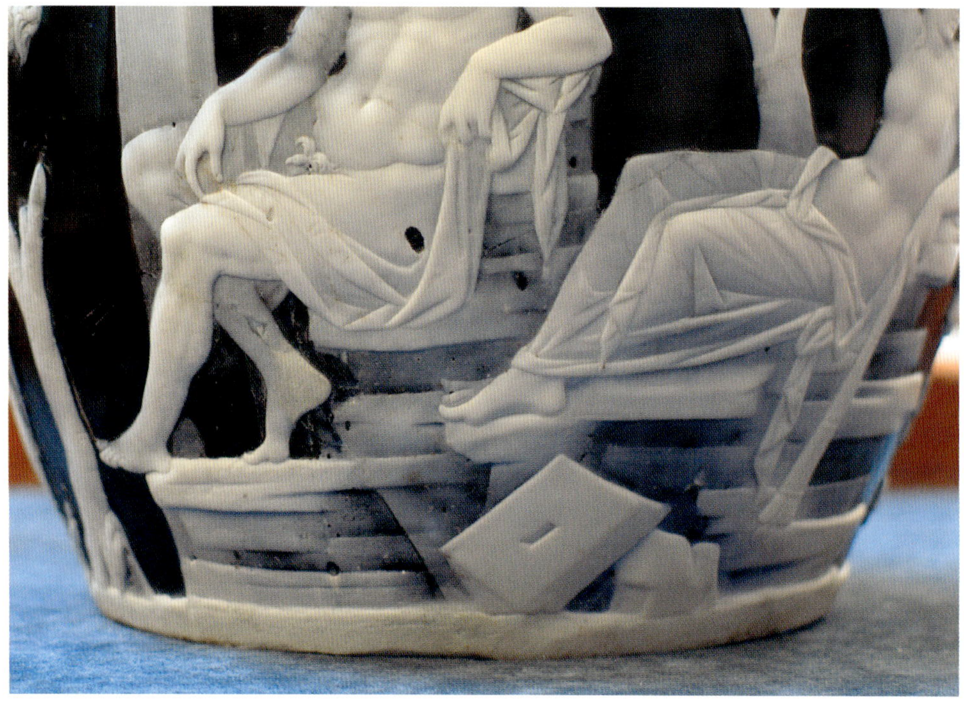

FIGURE 9
Detail of the Portland Vase, showing bubbles (e.g., on the thigh of the figure on the left).

Conversely, the cup-overlay method is just as likely *not* to trap bubbles between the two layers of glass (Figs. 10–18). The cup is formed by glassblowing, and therefore its inner surface is perfectly smooth. Then, when the molten glass is lowered into the cup, it drips off the end of the blowpipe and the cup is gradually filled. Air is safely and thoroughly pushed up and out of the narrowing crevice between the two glasses. Under these favorable conditions, there is little chance that bubbles will form.

In January and February 2007, at The Studio of The Corning Museum of Glass, I designed and carried out an experiment to test the supposition that the dip-overlay method tends to promote bubbles at the interface of the two glasses, while the cup-overlay method effectively avoids such bubbles. The two processes were repeated six times, using a high-quality colorless glass so that any bubbles located at the interface could be easily seen. The results were usually consistent with the pattern that we see in Roman-period objects, as compared with 19th-century English revival objects: many bubbles in the former, and few in the latter. Therefore, from both the historical and experimental evidence, we can reasonably conclude that there is an inherent, predictable, and important difference between these two processes—a difference that has a significant impact on the quality of the cameo glass blanks. While the dip-overlay method is much easier and quicker for the glassworker to execute, the cup-overlay method clearly results in superior blanks.

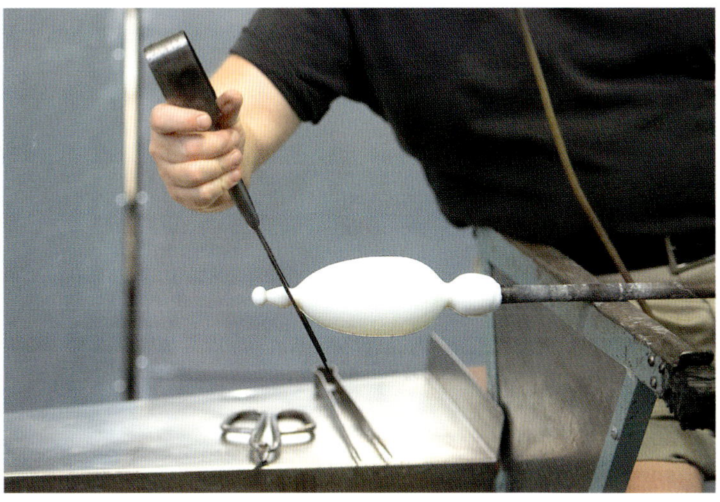

FIGURE 10
A cup of opaque white glass begins with a gather of glass on the end of a blowpipe. The glass is inflated, and a constriction is formed at each end.

FIGURE 11
After the excess glass has been knocked off the tip of the blowpipe, creating a hole, the glass is reheated in the furnace.

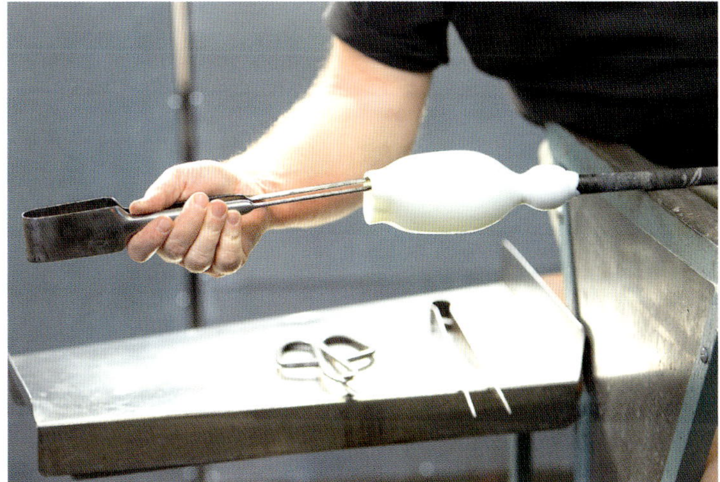

FIGURE 12
The hole is enlarged to create straight sides.

FIGURE 13
After the cup is freed from the blowpipe, it is placed upright on a stand in the kiln.

FIGURE 14
While the cup is kept hot (about 950°F or 510°C), blue glass is gathered on a blowpipe, then shaped and inflated to produce a parison.

FIGURE 15
More blue glass is gathered, and the parison is carefully positioned over the cup.

FIGURE 16
As the newly gathered blue glass starts to drip, it fills the bottom of the cup, pushing air upward and avoiding the trapping of bubbles.

FIGURE 17
The parison is further inflated to fill the cup.

FIGURE 18
After the glass is reheated in the furnace, it is inflated and shaped to create the body of the vessel.

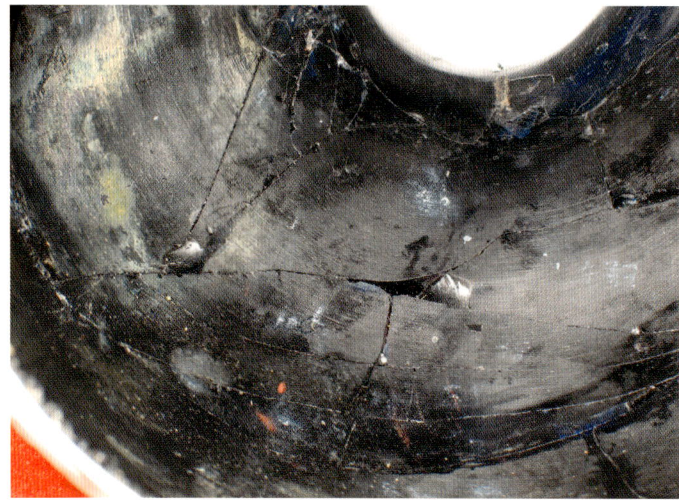

FIGURE 19
Interior of the Portland Vase, showing grinding marks.

In this context, it is interesting to note that a number of ancient cameo glass objects (including the Portland Vase, the Morgan Cup, and the Getty cup [**29**]) have more or less concentric grinding marks on the interior surface (Fig. 19). These were probably the by-product of an ingenious process used to detect large bubbles in the blue glass.[3] By grinding away some glass from the interior surface, glassmakers could locate and carefully note large bubbles within the vessel wall. Such bubbles, if accidentally encountered from the outside while the decoration was being cut, might easily destroy an object, costing the craftsmen hundreds of hours of work. This disaster could be averted by marking the location of large bubbles in the glass and then carefully avoiding any deep cutting in those areas.

The replicas of the Portland Vase made by John Northwood (1876; **33**) and Joseph Locke (1878; **35**) have no such internal grinding marks. Either these artisans did not understand the purpose and usefulness of the procedure, or perhaps they failed to notice the grinding marks on the object they were copying. On the other hand, they may have had such confidence in the quality of their glasses and in the cup-overlay method used to make the blanks that the threat of unwanted bubbles was not even considered. Rare as these bubbles must have been, we do have evidence that even in 19th-century England they were not an entirely unknown problem (Fig. 20).

While it is not difficult to learn how the overlay was achieved in the glasshouses that were active in the English revival of cameo glass, scholars have long been far less certain of the procedure that was used in antiquity. This matter now seems close to resolution.

---

3. A full explanation of the internal grinding procedure and its purpose will be published in Gudenrath and others forthcoming.

FIGURE 20

Unfinished Antony and Cleopatra *plaque. England, Amblecote, Thomas Webb & Sons, about 1895. D. 47.7 cm. The Corning Museum of Glass (89.2.6, gift of Juliette K. Rakow in memory of Dr. Leonard S. Rakow). Work was probably halted because the presence of a large bubble in the upper left portion of the object made the execution of the intended design impossible.*

The Reproduction of Roman Glass

Mark Taylor and David Hill

FOR ALMOST 20 YEARS, we have specialized in reproducing Roman glass, and we have tried to gain an understanding of the techniques and technology used by ancient glassworkers. This led us to conduct long-term experiments in building and using wood-fired furnaces, based on excavated material and the small amount of written and pictorial evidence from the Roman period. This is a summary of the techniques that we have evolved as a result of our study of ancient glass and our interaction with experts in this field.

Replicating the Composition and Properties of Roman Batch

Ancient glass has a soda-lime composition with a relatively high content of sodium oxide, which gives it comparatively low gathering temperatures of between 1020° and 1050°C.

A Roman batch for the production of transparent glass typically had two basic ingredients: sand and natron,[1] with ingredients such as calcium and aluminum present as impurities. The characteristic blue-green color of this glass was imparted by iron oxide, an impurity present in sand, although sources of relatively iron-free sand were known and exploited for the making of colorless glass.[2] Other materials, inten-

1. Natron is a naturally occurring form of sodium sesquicarbonate from the Wadi Natrun in Egypt.
2. Sources of glassmaking sand, such as the mouth of the Rivers Belus, on the eastern coast of the Mediterranean, and Volturnus, in southern Italy, are mentioned by Pliny (*Nat. Hist.* 36.65–66).

tionally added, gave various hues of blue, green, amber, brown, and purple to the glass.[3]

Modern raw materials allow us to replicate ancient glass recipes very accurately, and we can easily reproduce and assess the working properties of most transparent Roman glasses, based on published scientific analyses. However, opaque glasses, such as those used in mosaic vessels, differ in composition and can prove to be more difficult to re-create.[4]

Roman glass, in common with modern soda-lime glasses, tends to have a short working range,[5] and that of opaque and colored glasses is even shorter, forcing the craftsman to work quickly, constantly reheating his work. There are a few exceptions, such as some opaque white, opaque red, and opaque yellow glasses, whose compositions include lead. Lead serves to reduce the working temperature of the glass, the annealing temperature,[6] and the coefficient of expansion.[7] These properties are exploited in Roman cameo vessels, in which the addition of lead in the layer of white glass makes it easier to manipulate when it is hot. Lead has the added advantage of making the glass easier to cut and engrave when it is cold.

Core Forming and Slumping

Core forming is the process of coating a shaped core, attached to a metal rod, with hot glass to make the body of a vessel. Slumping is the process of allowing a flat glass sheet or disk to take the shape of a form, over which it is placed, under the influence of heat

---

3. Many modern scientific analyses of ancient glasses have been published (see, for example, Brill 1999). A typical composition of Roman glass is about 70% SiO_2, 18% Na_2O, 7% CaO, 2% Al_2O_3, <1% MgO, and <1% K_2O, with the remainder made up of small amounts of coloring oxides such as cobalt, copper, iron, and manganese, although manganese can be used as a decolorizer. Ancient glassmakers appear to have added these oxides as compounds and minerals.
4. Opaque colors such as white, yellow, red, and green have compositions that can be markedly different from those of transparent colors, and they can include high levels of antimony, lead, and copper oxides. Their production can involve two or even three stages.
5. The working range of a glass is its gathering temperature minus the temperature at which it becomes too difficult to work. In practice, this depends on the type of work being performed. Glassblowing, for instance, requires hotter temperatures than kiln forming.
6. The annealing temperature is the temperature at which glass will release its stresses without becoming distorted, and annealing is the process that removes these stresses, which would become locked in the glass if it cools too quickly.
7. The coefficient of expansion of each glass is an important consideration when fusing two or more glasses, as in mosaic and cameo glass. Different coefficients of expansion will result in different rates of shrinkage upon cooling, stressing the finished vessel and leading to cracks and breakage. Annealing temperatures and coefficients of expansion must be addressed when calculating batch compositions.

and gravity. These are two of the principal methods of creating glass vessels that were used before the discovery of glassblowing in the middle of the first century B.C.

The cores and forms appear to have been made of clay mixed with an organic material such as finely chopped hay, or chaff from the threshing floor. This core material is easily shaped by hand. It can be molded or thrown, pressed into bowls or other open shapes, or formed into the shape of a vessel at one end of a metal gathering rod. If enough organic material is included, the mixture becomes highly resistant to thermal shock, and it can be heated rapidly to fire the clay and burn away the organic matter. This creates a network of tiny holes, linked by small bridges of fired clay, which allows the core to be crushed as the cooling glass vessel shrinks around it, preventing breakage.

Hot glass will adhere to this core material. This is a useful property during shaping because it permits the glass to be manipulated, and it helps to steady the vessel while it is being formed. It leaves a rough surface on the inside of the vessel, which can be ground away later.

Making Mosaic Glass Canes

Mosaic glass is made of multicolored glass canes that are used either as flat lengths or as short, circular cross sections that show the pattern to its best effect. These canes can be made by a single glassworker with two or more pots of compatible[8] molten glass of different colors.

Before a cane is pulled to the desired length, the pattern is created in hot glass on a gathering rod. We use several basic hot-forming techniques to accomplish this, including the gathering of successive layers of glass (either concentrically or in specific areas on the previous gather), scraping away the excess glass, adding a trail of a contrasting color, flattening the glass to form a "tongue," and stretching and coiling flattened lengths of bicolored glass. When these techniques are combined with preformed canes, which we cut, reheat, and fuse together, we are able to produce more complex patterns.

The completed design is pulled to form a cane of the correct diameter (or width, if it is a flat cane). Twisting the glass rapidly while it is being stretched produces a tight spiral that runs along the cane. This pattern is often seen on the rims of mosaic bowls, and it is usually referred to as a "network cane." Success in pulling a cane depends on the correct and thorough reheating of the gather. After the canes are annealed, they are cut into smaller segments in order to make mosaic vessels, although they may also be used for inlays on furniture or walls.

8. Compatible glasses have the same coefficient of expansion. See note 7.

Making Mosaic Glass Vessels (75)

Our mosaic vessels begin with the formation of a flat disk of glass. Most disks are formed by assembling precut strips and sections of canes on a ceramic surface, which we heat to working temperatures (about 1000°–1050°C) to allow us to fuse and manipulate the glass with metal hand tools. The hot disk is transferred to an upturned form, the shape of which will become that of the inside of the vessel, and allowed to slump. This process must be controlled with careful heating and manipulation. We can add a separate preformed foot-ring at this stage, if one is desired.

There are several variations of the technique for hot-forming the initial disk. These include bending and winding the canes as they are heated in order to form meandering and spiral patterns, and adding individual sections to the surface of a disk to form inlaid patterns. A network cane can be fused to the rim of the disk, or an integral foot can be formed by filling a hollow ring in the ceramic surface with cane sections as part of the assembly process.

After the vessel has been annealed, we remove the cold ceramic form, use hard sandstone to grind the coarse inside surface smooth, and polish it with pumice. The simplest method of grinding involves mounting the vessel centrally on a horizontal wheel and rotating it while applying the abrasives, using water to keep the glass cool. The concentric scratches that are often seen inside ancient vessels are evidence of this process.

Making Ribbed Bowls

Ribbed bowls are made in a similar manner to mosaic vessels, but the former require hot disks decorated with radiating ribs. The disks may be fashioned from mosaic glass, but monochrome bowls are quicker to make.

To create a disk for a monochrome ribbed bowl, we flatten a large gather of hot glass with a heavy, damp wooden block. The glass must be constantly reheated to allow us to raise each rib individually by squeezing the glass with pincers and then flattening the wider end with a blade. After it is pinched, the disk is slumped over a form.

The various sizes and shapes of ribs on ancient bowls, together with their frequently uneven spacing, provide strong evidence that Roman glassmakers pinched the ribs of their vessels. Some ribs include details such as undercutting, which could have been formed only by pinching from above, and some have a softer outline caused by several reheatings.

After the bowl has been annealed, its interior is ground and polished, and decorative rings may be added by cutting. In most cases, the grinding includes the lip and the outside rim above the tops of the ribs, removing tool marks that were produced while the glass was being formed.

Working as a team of two, we have been able to make both mosaic and monochrome ribbed bowls in wood-fired furnaces with a sandstone slab that forms a wide table in front of the gathering hole. Using a tool with a long metal handle, we can easily slide the disk in and out of the furnace, and the disk can be manipulated on the table while both workers remain a comfortable distance from the heat.

Making Blown Glass Vessels

The only ancient depiction of glassblowing is found on three lamps that date to the first century A.D.[9] They show a glassmaker blowing a vessel while seated on a stool in front of a wood-fired furnace. Crouching nearby is an assistant who may have been responsible for stoking the furnace and for helping the glassblower in other ways.

The few surviving tools, together with evidence from Roman vessels and waste glass, show that most of the traditional wooden and metal glassworking tools were employed in antiquity. One exception is cross-bladed shears, since we know that handles and applied masks were cast off rather than sheared.

Our work with wood-fired furnaces demonstrates that the style of glassblowing illustrated on the lamps is well suited to the blowing of lightweight, small to medium-sized vessels. Blowing and gathering irons can rest on the thighs (using lengths of flat wood for protection from the heat), and vessels can easily be reheated in the gathering hole, employing a small rest for the iron. An assistant can help with the addition of handles, trailed decoration, and puntying, but even these tasks can be performed unaided.

With tools situated close to hand and the marver in front of the furnace, the glassblower may work quickly and economically. This is a comfortable, convenient style, suitable both for blowing and for mold blowing (see below). The only real disadvantage is the exposure to smoke and excess heat, particularly if one is working in an enclosed area.

Mold Blowing and Moldmaking (**113** and **114**)

The use of molds developed soon after glassblowing was discovered. Two types of molds evolved: open molds for straight-sided storage vessels, and closed, multipart molds for more elaborate decorated vessels.

Surviving fragments show that open molds were made from stone or fired ceramic slabs arranged upright around a square, hexagonal, or rectangular base block that was often engraved with concentric rings or other designs.

---

9. The three lamps are from Asseria, in the Museum of Archeology, Split, Croatia (1094-30); from Voghenza, in the National Museum of Archeology, Ferrara, Italy (52196); and from Spodnje Škofije, in the Piran Archaeological Museum, Slovenia (PN A 270). The last of these is a recent find, and it shows the clearest detail.

Open molds can be reproduced in a straightforward manner. However, no examples of Roman multipart molds have yet been found, so we have based ours on a close study of surviving vessels. These offer clues about the mold material, its thickness, and the number of segments, and they suggest that fired ceramic was the most likely fabric for mold construction in antiquity.

We mold damp clay around a lathe-turned form and cut it away to create the side and base panels. The decoration is incised into each part with simple tools. The completed molds are fired, and their inner surfaces are coated with a layer of soot that acts as a "separator." Short handles permit us to use these molds with gloved hands.

Mold blowing involves creating a blown parison, shaping it to fit into the mold, and evenly distributing the glass as it is inflated. The glassblower can use open molds unaided, but an assistant is needed to open and close multipart molds.

For beakers, the dome at the top of the blown vessel (the moil) is removed after annealing, but other vessels are either puntied or gripped, allowing the glassblower to shape necks and rims, and to add handles.

Observations on Roman Glassworking

When studying ancient glass vessels and waste glass for evidence of manufacturing techniques, one notices crossover, adaptation, and evolution in hot glassworking. A good example of this is the range of small, highly colored bottles dating from shortly after the advent of glassblowing. These hybrids appear to have been made by attaching small fused mosaic strips, disks, or cups to a blowing iron and inflating them.

Both vessels and waste glass show that many of the tools for glassblowing would already have been in use: gathering rods, wooden sticks and boards, pincers and tweezers, and marvers. A series of core-formed mosaic glass bottles with pulled-out bases and shaped base-knobs, dating from the second century B.C., may indicate the use of U-shaped tools.

All of the hot-forming methods described above require molten glass that is fluid enough to be gathered and shaped. Our work has shown that small wood-fired furnaces are easily able to reach temperatures well above 1000°C, and, with effort, they can be coaxed above 1120°C. The making of mosaic and ribbed bowls becomes easier at temperatures close to 1100°C, and ribs can be formed only after the glass becomes sufficiently fluid to be pinched. Tool marks on the outer surfaces of these bowls show that the glassworker needed to pull the hot glass into shape as it was slumped.

The discovery of blowing freed the glassworker from the limitations of using cores and forms, and the time-consuming work of removing the core and polishing the vessel became unnecessary. Existing glass-forming techniques were adapted, production increased rapidly, and a great variety of shapes quickly evolved. Mold blowing, in particular, allowed large numbers of vessels to be made in a very short time.

Blowing rapidly became the main form of glass production, although some early blown forms and decorations reflected older styles and tastes. Pinched ribs decorated small flasks, jugs, bowls, and jars, and splashed decoration imitated mosaic glass. A particular feature of glassblowing is its spontaneity. New forms and designs can develop very quickly, although practicality and popularity will often affect their longevity. This, coupled with the freedom of manipulation that glassblowing offers the skilled craftsman, helps to account for the enormous proliferation of shapes and decorations within Roman blown glass.

As is revealed by the high quality of much of their work, Roman glassmakers had become highly skilled in manipulating hot glass, a material that must be handled with respect and care. Specialization inevitably ensued, and particular types of vessels became associated with certain areas and perhaps even with individual workshops. Examples include mosaic vessels with specific styles of patterning, early mold-blown vessels that bore the maker's or workshop owner's name as part of the decoration, and workshops that focused on the production of objects requiring large quantities of glass, such as windowpanes and mold-blown bottles.

The techniques developed by ancient glassmakers are evident in all of the handworked glass from later periods, and they continue to evolve in modern glassworking. In our study of these techniques, the most important observation we have made, by far, is that the simplest solution to a given problem is the one that is most likely to have been adopted.

CATALOG

A. *Historismus*
Roman Originals

1. Beaker

Roman Empire, first century A.D.
H. 9.3 cm, D. (body) 7.7 cm
Glass blown into silver beaker; rim of glass ground
The British Museum, London (GR 1870.9–.12)

The records of The British Museum state that the beaker was acquired in Florence, Italy. The beaker itself has a label indicating that it came from Brindisi in 1865. The challenge of inflating a glass vessel inside a metal casing appealed to modern glassmakers, who reproduced this vessel with both red and blue glass liners.

BIBLIOGRAPHY: *Glass of the Caesars* 1987, pp. 153–154 and 156, no. 78.

2. Jar with Lid

Roman Empire, first to second century A.D.
OH. 30.1 cm
Blown
The Corning Museum of Glass (70.1.44)
Formerly in the collection of Dr. Joseph W. Hambuechen

Many objects of this type have been found in Germany, but examples are known from Pompeii, Italy (buried no later than A.D. 79), southern France, and England. The weathering and encrustation on the jar, which are most evident on the lower part of the interior, may indicate that the vessel was used as a cinerary urn and that the encrustation is derived from the cremated bones.

BIBLIOGRAPHY: Whitehouse 1997, p. 174, no. 305.

Modern Imitations

3. Beaker

Italy, late 19th century, probably after 1879
H. 10.2 cm, D. (max.) 7.6 cm
Glass blown into metal beaker; rim of glass ground
The Corning Museum of Glass (59.3.37)
Formerly in the collection of Ray Winfield Smith

This is a simplified copy of **1**. The first known publication of that object was in 1879, and imitations may have been made shortly after that date.

BIBLIOGRAPHY: Whitehouse 2003, pp. 92–93, no. 1040.

4. Urn

Italy, Venice, Compagnia di Venezia e Murano (C.V.M.), about 1881
H. 40.5 cm
Blown
Collection of Rainer Zietz, London

This is a 19th-century copy of a Roman cinerary urn. An identical vessel appears in an engraving of the C.V.M. exhibit at the 1881 Esposizione Industriale Italiana in Milan.

Imitation of Byzantine Original

5. Painted Bowl

Italy, Venice, Compagnia di Venezia e Murano (signed "C.V.M."), probably about 1878
H. 10.3 cm, D. (max.) 19.3 cm
Blown, enameled, gilded
The Corning Museum of Glass (59.3.36)
Formerly in the collection of Ray Winfield Smith

This is a careful copy of a bowl with gilded, enameled, and silver-stained decoration in the Treasury of San Marco, Venice. The original was made, probably in Constantinople, in the 10th century (Gudenrath and others 2007).

BIBLIOGRAPHY: Buckton and others 1984, pp. 180–183, no. 21.

Imitations of Medieval Islamic Originals

6. Lamp

France, Paris, decorated by Philippe-Joseph Brocard (1831–1896), about 1870–1880
H. 31.7 cm, D. (max.) 24 cm
Blown (from two gathers), enameled, gilded
The Corning Museum of Glass (78.3.16, gift of Mr. and Mrs. Arthur Appleton)

The first glass objects to replicate the medieval Islamic style of ornamentation were made by the Imperial Glass Factory of St. Petersburg, Russia, and shown at the 1867 world's fair in Paris. At the 1873 fair in Vienna, the Russian factory was joined by J. & L. Lobmeyr of Vienna and Philippe-Joseph Brocard of Paris in displaying Islamic-style enameled glass. Lobmeyr maintained that Brocard had contributed "the most beautiful [examples] of this kind in the exhibition" (Spiegl 1980, p. 261). For additional information on Brocard, Lobmeyr, and other glassmakers at the world's fairs, see *Glass of the Sultans* 2001, pp. 297–301.

BIBLIOGRAPHY: *Glass of the Sultans* 2001, p. 307, no. 154.

7. Hanging Lamp

France, Nancy, Emile Gallé (1846–1904), about 1884
H. 21.6 cm, D. (max.) 15.2 cm
Blown (from two gathers), applied, acid-etched, iridized, stained, enameled, gilded
The Corning Museum of Glass (69.3.9)

This hanging lamp is a tour de force of glassmaking. It exhibits an extraordinary range of decorative techniques. The decoration was executed with great precision. The figures in the medallions may have been copied from 19th-century Iranian manuscripts or metalwork. Emile Gallé began to experiment with enamels about 1873, and within a year, he had perfected a wide range of colors.

BIBLIOGRAPHY: *Glass of the Sultans* 2001, pp. 308–309, no. 155.

8. Covered Vase

Austria, Vienna, J. & L. Lobmeyr, designed by Franz Schmoranz (1845–1892) and Johann Machytka (1845–1886?) in 1876
OH. 32.2 cm, H. (vase) 27.1 cm, D. (max.) 15.9 cm
Blown, enameled, gilded
The Corning Museum of Glass (73.3.18)

The Bohemian architects Franz and Gustav Schmoranz were keenly interested in medieval Islamic art. Franz helped to design this vase, while his brother published the first comprehensive account of medieval Near Eastern glassmaking.

9. Beaker

France, probably Paris, late 19th century
H. 10.5 cm, D. (max.) 9.3 cm
Blown, gilded, enameled, cut
The Corning Museum of Glass (69.3.67, gift of Jerome Strauss)
Formerly in the collection of Jerome Strauss

This beaker is somewhat similar in form to the Palmer Cup in The British Museum, London. Although Philippe-Joseph Brocard (1831–1896) was the best-known glass enameler at the time the Corning vessel was made, there were other workshops in Paris, such as those of J. Philippe Imberton (active 1880–1890) and Albert Pfulb (active 1865–1888). Therefore, we cannot be sure who made this remarkable beaker.

BIBLIOGRAPHY: *Glass Drinking Vessels* 1955, p. 137, no. 352.

Imitations of European Medieval and Renaissance Originals

10. Covered *Daumenglas*

Probably Germany, possibly Ehrenfeld, Rheinische Glashütten A.G., about 1880
OH. 36.8 cm, H. (vessel) 27.3 cm, D. (max.) 19 cm
Blown, applied
The Corning Museum of Glass (56.3.64)

This vessel copies barrel-shaped *Daumengläser* (thumb glasses) that were popular in Germany and the Netherlands in the 16th and 17th centuries. The thumb holes helped drinkers to grip the vessels securely.

11. Tumbler

Probably Germany, late 19th century
H. 7.7 cm, D. (rim) 7.8 cm
Blown, dip-molded
The Corning Museum of Glass (53.3.24A)

This tumbler imitates German ribbed beakers of the 15th century.

12. Prunted Beaker

Probably Germany, late 19th century
H. 27.4 cm, D. (max.) 14.5 cm
Blown, applied
The Corning Museum of Glass (75.3.25)
Formerly in the collection of Jacques Mühsam

At the time this beaker was made, there were many glasshouses in Germany and Bohemia that produced imitations of late medieval *Waldglas* (forest glass), including the Rheinische Glashütten A.G. in Ehrenfeld, Germany, and the Theresienthal crystal glass factory in the Bavarian Forest.

13. Goblet

Germany, 19th century
H. 16.5 cm, D. (rim) 11.2 cm
Blown, applied
The Corning Museum of Glass (56.3.92)
Formerly in the Eigel Collection

The design of this vessel is somewhat influenced by stemmed cups of the first half of the 16th century.

14. Stangenglas

Germany, Ehrenfeld, Rheinische Glashütten A.G., about 1886
H. 25.3 cm, D. (max.) 9.4 cm
Blown, trailed, prunted
The Corning Museum of Glass (76.3.38, gift of Jerome Strauss)
Formerly in the collection of Jerome Strauss

This vessel was made in imitation of German or Swiss *Stangengläser* of the late 15th or early 16th century (cf. *Phönix aus Sand und Asche* 1988, pp. 392–395, nos. 491–494). The entire production of the Rheinische Glashütten was based on historic glass vessels. In meticulously copying the shape and color of these objects, the company expressed its deep admiration of the past. The aim was not merely to equal the skills of earlier glassmakers, but to surpass them with superb craftsmanship, employing the advanced technology of the late 19th century. For the design of this *Stangenglas*, named "Erwin-Humpen," see Schäfke 1979, pp. 104–105, no. 112.

Imitations of Venetian Renaissance Originals

15. Copy of the Coppa Barovier

Italy, Venice, Compagnia di Venezia e Murano (C.V.M.), probably about 1878
H. 18 cm, D. (rim) 21.3 cm
Blown, enameled
The Corning Museum of Glass (70.3.1)

This object was made in imitation of the famous 15th-century Venetian marriage goblet in the Museo del Vetro, Murano. A similar bowl was displayed at the 1878 world's fair in Paris.

16. Goblet

Italy, Venice, Compagnia di Venezia e Murano (C.V.M.), about 1878
H. 25 cm, D. (foot) 12.3 cm
Blown, enameled
The Corning Museum of Glass (79.3.339, gift of The Ruth Bryan Strauss Memorial Foundation)
Formerly in the collection of Jerome Strauss

A well-known marriage goblet made in Venice during the 15th century was the model for this glass. The original is part of the Slade Collection at The British Museum, London. This copy or a similar glass was displayed at the 1878 world's fair in Paris.

BIBLIOGRAPHY: Spillman 1981, p. 36, fig. 2.

17. Footed Beaker

Italy, Venice, enameled by Francesco Toso Borella (1846–1905; signed), after 1871
H. 13.9 cm, D. (rim) 9.8 cm
Blown, enameled
The Corning Museum of Glass (74.3.123)

Francesco Toso Borella was a leading Muranese decorator. The beaker is a reproduction, in part, of a Renaissance goblet in The British Museum, London (Slade Collection, S. 391; see Tait 1979, pp. 32–33, no. 13). The copy lacks the male figure that appears on the reverse of the Slade glass, so it was probably produced on the basis of an illustration rather than an examination of the original vessel.

18. *Lattimo* Flask

Italy, Venice, about 1880–1930
H. 18.3 cm, W. (max.) 11.2 cm
Blown, enameled
The Corning Museum of Glass (75.3.70)

This is a close copy of an early 16th-century bottle that was stolen from the Museo Vetrario (now the Museo del Vetro), Murano, in 1955. The theft is particularly regrettable because only about a dozen Renaissance *lattimo* glasses are known to exist, including one closely related bottle in The Walters Art Gallery, Baltimore (cf. Clarke 1974, figs. 9 and 10). The copy provides a three-dimensional impression of what the original looked like.

One side of the bottle shows Cupid fishing, and the other portrays Venus and Mars. Both scenes are allegories of the conquests of love.

19. *Nef* (Aquamanile) in the Form of a Boat

Italy, Venice, Salviati and Company, about 1870
H. 19.3 cm, W. (max.) 14.6 cm
Blown, pattern-molded, applied
The Corning Museum of Glass (59.3.24)

In his diary of 1525, the chronicler Martin Sanudo (1466–1536) mentions that he had seen boat-shaped aquamaniles at the Fair of the Ascension in Venice. Such vessels were the models for objects like this. The boat was published as no. 1051 in a Salviati and Company design book.

Imitations of *Façon de Venise* Originals

20. Covered Winged Goblet

Germany, Hamburg, probably workshop of C. H. F. Müller, probably designed by Hermann Robert Bichweiler (1849–1915), about 1870–1880
OH. 40.9 cm, H. (goblet) 26 cm, D. (max.) 9.1 cm
Lampworked
The Corning Museum of Glass (59.3.47)

From about 1865 to the 1880s, Carl Heinrich Florenz Müller (1845–1912) made lampworked glass vessels in historical styles. Among them was this vessel, which is based on 17th-century Dutch winged goblets. Müller excelled in copying antique glasses in Venetian style, which were soon sold by unscrupulous German and Dutch dealers as antique originals. Later works, such as the tall flute glasses, were freer interpretations of Venetian prototypes. Müller finally turned to the making of electrical equipment, a new technology, and he produced some of the first X-ray tubes.

BIBLIOGRAPHY: Ricke 1978, pp. 91–92, no. III 2, fig. 43.

21. Serpent-Stem Goblet

Germany, Hamburg, C. H. F. Müller (1845–1912), about 1865–1870
H. 27 cm, D. (max.) 10.3 cm
Blown, trailed, applied
The Corning Museum of Glass (72.3.36, gift of Jerome Strauss)

See **20**.

BIBLIOGRAPHY: Ricke 1978, p. 70, no. 11d.

Modern Imitations of Antique European Glasses

22. Reichsadlerhumpen

Central Europe, late 19th century
H. 32.6 cm, D. (max.) 15.2 cm
Blown, enameled, gilded
The Corning Museum of Glass (57.3.60, gift of Edwin J. Beinecke)

Vessels such as this are almost indistinguishable from their 16th- and 17th-century models. Fritz Heckert (1837–1887) in Petersdorf, Silesia, and other manufacturers took great pride in the fidelity of their replicas to the originals.

BIBLIOGRAPHY: *Beinecke Collection* 1965, p. 270, no. 18.

23. Goblet with Apollo and the Muses

Bohemia, late 19th century
H. 20.6 cm, D. (foot) 10.5 cm
Blown, cut, engraved
The Corning Museum of Glass (86.3.85, gift of Mrs. K. F. Landegger)

In shape as well as in decoration, this goblet stands in the tradition of Bohemian engraved glasses of the early 18th century. Seldom, however, would an 18th-century Bohemian glass engraver have created such an elaborate figural design.

24. Covered Goblet

Bohemia, Adolfshütte/Adolfov, Meyr's Neffe glassworks, about 1890
OH. 33.6 cm, H. (goblet) 22.3 cm, D. (max.) 9.5 cm
Blown, cut, gilded, enameled
The Corning Museum of Glass (53.3.11)

The painting in gold and *Schwarzlot* (black lead), a sepia enamel that was first used on stained glass, was characteristic of the work of the Silesian artist Ignaz Preissler (1676–1741). This covered goblet is decorated with an imitation of Preissler's style of painting.

BIBLIOGRAPHY: *Guide to the Collections* 1958, p. 59, no. 65.

25. Covered Goblet with Enameled Monograms

Central Europe, perhaps Silesia, Josephinenhütte, probably 19th century
OH. 30.8 cm, H. (goblet) 19.5 cm, D. (foot) 9.9 cm
Blown, gilded, enameled
The Corning Museum of Glass (72.3.33, gift of Jerome Strauss)

This is a puzzling object. If it is a 19th-century goblet, it imitates northern German or Saxon goblets of the mid-18th century. The enameling is highly unusual for both the 18th and 19th centuries. There seems to be a double pontil mark, indicating that the enamels were furnace-fired. This technique became obsolete when the kiln-firing of enamels on glass was introduced in the late 19th century. The bowl and the cover show incipient crizzling, which is also uncommon with late 19th-century glass. However, the excellent condition of the gilding, as well as the design of the cartouches, speaks in favor of a 19th-century dating.

26. Ruby-Stained Goblet

Bohemia, probably Haida/Nový Bor, Friedrich Egermann (1777–1864), about 1850–1860
OH. 31.5 cm, H. (goblet) 21 cm, D. (max.) 10.6 cm
Blown, ruby-stained, engraved
The Corning Museum of Glass (79.3.845, gift of The Ruth Bryan Strauss Memorial Foundation)

This glass is similar, in shape and decoration, to Rococo-period goblets of about 1750. The ruby color, however, resembles that of gold ruby glasses made at the turn of the 17th century.

B. Cameo Glass
Roman Originals

27. Portland Vase Base Disk

Roman Empire, 25 B.C.–A.D. 25
D. 12.2 cm
Cast (in two layers, opaque white over translucent blue), carved, cut, polished
The British Museum, London (GR 1945.9-27.2)

This disk, which was inserted face downward, cannot be the original base of the Portland Vase: (1) the colors of the blue glass do not match, (2) the white glass differs in composition, (3) the figure and foliage on the disk are not by the same hand as the frieze on the vase, and (4) the disk was cut from a larger composition. Nevertheless, the disk already formed the base of the vase in 1635, and it is very likely that it was attached in antiquity. Modern analysis of the Portland Vase, in particular the elongation of the bubbles preserved in the lower body, suggests that when the vase was first manufactured, it was shaped as an amphora with a pointed base (cf. **38** and **39**). At an unknown date, but probably in antiquity, the base of the vessel was damaged and the replacement disk was inserted.

BIBLIOGRAPHY: Glass of the Caesars 1987, pp. 66–67, no. 30; Gudenrath, Painter, and Whitehouse 1990, pp. 21–23.

28. AULDJO JUG

Roman Empire, 25 B.C.–A.D. 25
H. (with handle) 22.8 cm, D. (body) 14.3 cm
Blown, cased (dip-overlay method, opaque white over translucent blue), carved, cut, ground, polished
The British Museum, London (GR 1840.12-15.41, 1859.2-16.1)

This object was found between 1830 and 1832 in the House of the Faun in Pompeii, Italy. Chemical analysis has established that the opaque white glass has a high (23%) lead content, contrasting with 12% in the Portland Vase. The presence of lead in the glass would have made it softer and therefore easier to carve. That the handle was dropped onto the shoulder is suggested by the distortion at the point of attachment.

BIBLIOGRAPHY: *Glass of the Caesars* 1987, p. 79, no. 34; Painter and Whitehouse 1990a, pp. 149–150, figs. 109 and 110.

29. Cup

Roman Empire, 25 B.C.–A.D. 25
H. 10.5 cm, W. 17.6 cm
Probably cast; cased (dip-overlay method, opaque white over translucent blue), carved, cut, ground, polished
The J. Paul Getty Museum, Malibu, California (JPGM 84.AF.85)

The quality of the carving on this cup ranges from the sure treatment of the drapery and musculature to errors of proportion that are especially marked in the figure leaning on a krater. Several elements are reminiscent of the Portland Vase. The Bacchic imagery is appropriate for a vessel that was used for drinking wine.

BIBLIOGRAPHY: Painter and Whitehouse 1990a, pp. 143–145, no. A4; Whitehouse 1991, pp. 25, 27, and 31, no. 16; Wight 2003.

30. Flask

Roman Empire, 25 B.C.–A.D. 25
H. 7.6 cm, W. 4.2 cm
Blown, cased (dip-overlay method, opaque white over translucent blue), carved, cut, ground, polished
The J. Paul Getty Museum, Malibu, California (JPGM 85.AF.84)
Formerly in the collection of Ernst Kofler and Marthe Truniger

While scholars have offered various interpretations of the frieze that decorates this perfume flask, Bianchi (1988) doubts that the figures have any special significance. "The vignettes could be nothing more than a simple allusion to Egypt as the source of the perfume that was originally contained in this vessel," he wrote. "As a luxury item, it could very well reflect the pretentious affectations of some wealthy, but boorish, Campanian devotee of an Egyptian cult."

BIBLIOGRAPHY: *Glass of the Caesars* 1987, pp. 53–57 and 83–84, no. 36; Painter and Whitehouse 1990a, pp. 150–153, no. A8; Whitehouse 1991, no. 13.

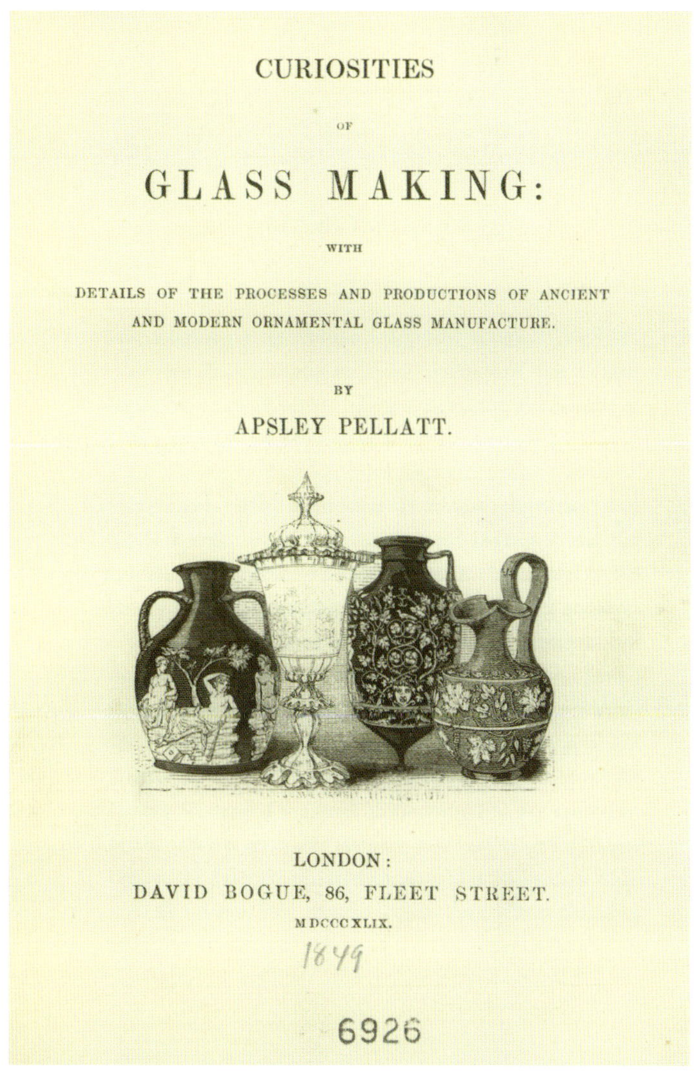
CURIOSITIES

OF

GLASS MAKING:

WITH

DETAILS OF THE PROCESSES AND PRODUCTIONS OF ANCIENT AND MODERN ORNAMENTAL GLASS MANUFACTURE.

BY

APSLEY PELLATT.

LONDON:
DAVID BOGUE, 86, FLEET STREET.
MDCCCXLIX.

31. *Curiosities of Glass Making . . .*

Apsley Pellatt, Curiosities of Glass Making: With Details of the Processes and Productions of Ancient and Modern Ornamental Glass Manufacture, *London: David Bogue, 1849*

(a) Research Library, Getty Research Institute, Los Angeles, California (87-B14030) [Shown in Malibu only.]

(b) Rakow Research Library, The Corning Museum of Glass (28365) [Shown in Corning only.]

Apsley Pellatt II (1791–1863) was the proprietor of the Falcon Glass House in Blackfriars, London. He had a keen interest in the chemistry of glass, and he built a laboratory for experiments with optical glass. *Curiosities of Glass Making* was based on a series of lectures he delivered at London's Royal Institution in 1848.

Modern Imitations

32. Ceramic Replica of the Portland Vase

England, Etruria, Josiah Wedgwood (1730–1795), about 1790
H. 26 cm, D. (max.) 18.6 cm
Stoneware
Vessel thrown, handles applied, decoration molded and applied; ground, polished
The Corning Museum of Glass (92.7.2, purchased with funds from the Clara S. Peck Endowment)
Formerly in the collection of Dr. and Mrs. Leonard S. Rakow

Josiah Wedgwood was a remarkable English potter who introduced many new forms that were frequently based on classical models. In the early 1770s, he began to experiment with jasperware, a fine-grained stoneware that can be stained. This "first edition" copy of the Portland Vase was purchased by Richard Barker, a friend of Wedgwood's business partner. The fame of the Portland Vase and of Wedgwood's ceramic replicas helped to establish cameo glass making in England.

BIBLIOGRAPHY: Whitehouse 2003, pp. 177–178, no. 1202.

33. Replica of the Portland Vase

England, Wordsley, Red House Glass Works, John Northwood (1836–1902), 1873–1876
H. 25 cm, D. (max.) 18.2 cm
Blown, cased (cup-overlay method, opaque white over translucent blue), acid-dipped, carved, ground, polished
The Corning Museum of Glass (92.2.7, bequest of Juliette K. Rakow)
Formerly in the collections of the Pargeter family, E. Mary Duffy, and Dr. and Mrs. Leonard S. Rakow
[Shown in Corning only.]

In 1873, Philip Pargeter, proprietor of the Red House Glass Works, told John Northwood, "I believe I can make the Portland Vase if you can decorate it." Northwood accepted the challenge, and he spent three years carving his replica. At an advanced stage, the vase cracked as a result of thermal shock. Fortunately, the crack was repaired with an adhesive, and Northwood completed his task. Frederick Carder said he was inspired to work with glass rather than with pottery when he saw Northwood's reproduction of the Portland Vase.

BIBLIOGRAPHY: Whitehouse 2003, pp. 86–88, no. 1032.

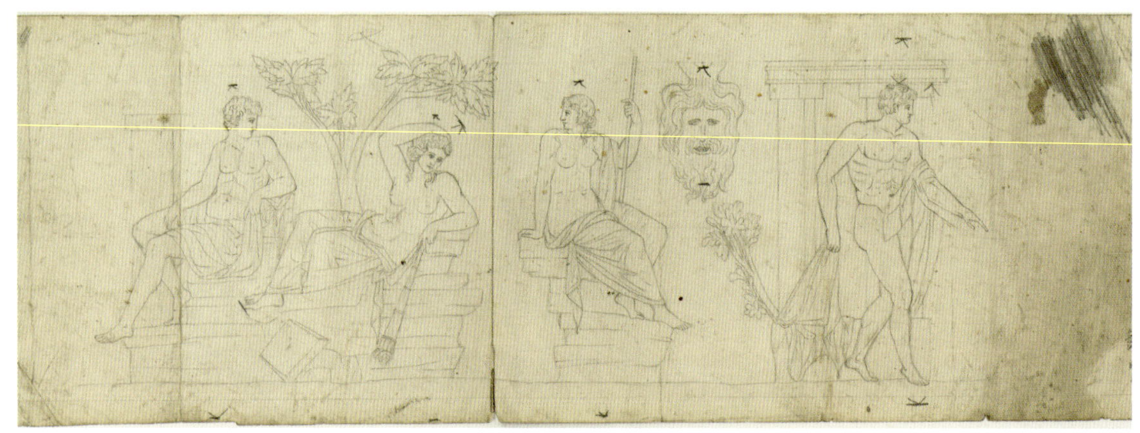

34. Study of Figures on the Portland Vase

England, Wordsley, John Northwood (1836–1902), 1873
H. 16.5 cm
Pencil on paper
Rakow Research Library, The Corning Museum of Glass (89966)

John Northwood made this detailed drawing of the figural composition on the Portland Vase before he began to make his replica, a project that required three years to complete. He carefully marked the dimensions of each of the figures on the drawing so that he could transfer this information onto the blank from which he engraved the scene.

BIBLIOGRAPHY: *Cameo Glass* 1982, pp. 44–45, fig. 17.

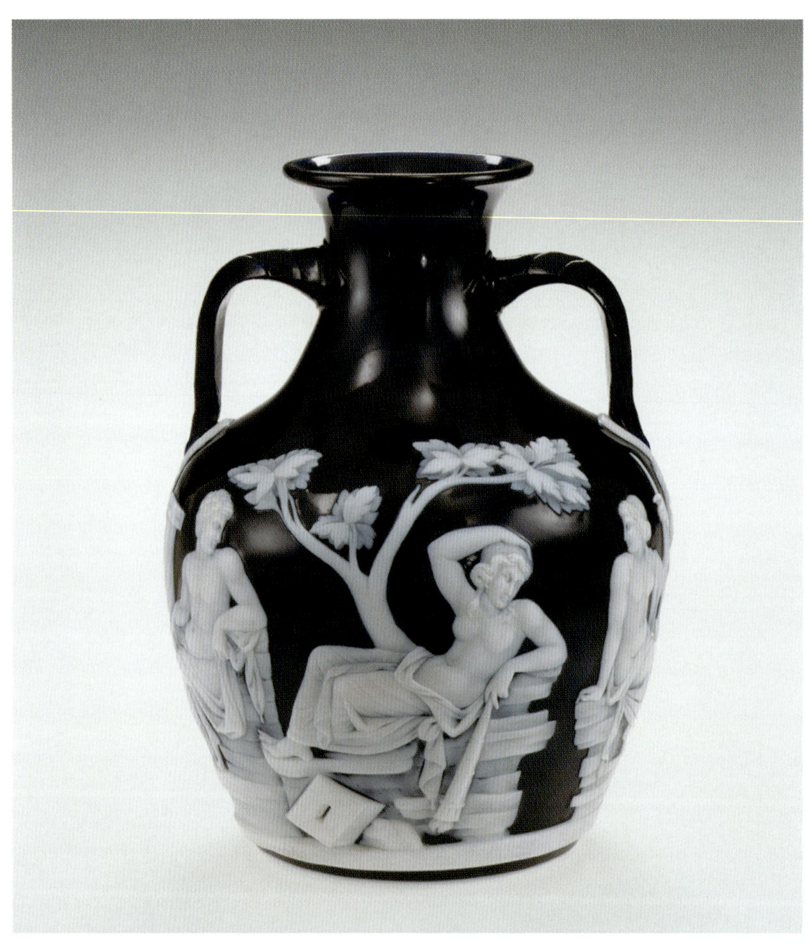

35. Replica of the Portland Vase

England, Wordsley, Hodgetts, Richardson and Son, Joseph Locke (1846–1936), 1878
H. 25 cm, D. (max.) 9.7 cm
Blown, cased (cup-overlay method, opaque white over translucent blue), acid-dipped, carved, ground, polished
The Corning Museum of Glass (92.2.15, purchased with funds from the Clara S. Peck Endowment)
Formerly in the collection of Dr. and Mrs. Leonard S. Rakow

Joseph Locke was commissioned to make this copy of the Portland Vase for display at the 1878 world's fair in Paris. He worked on his replica for almost a year, and although it was unfinished at the time of the exposition, it won him a silver medal. He never completed the thinning of the figures on the vase.

BIBLIOGRAPHY: Whitehouse 2003, pp. 88–89, no. 1033.

36. Portland Vase Blank

England, Wordsley, Hodgetts, Richardson and Son, 1878
H. 25.3 cm, D. (rim) 10 cm
Blown, cased (cup-overlay method, opaque white over translucent blue)
The Corning Museum of Glass (92.2.16, purchased with funds from the Clara S. Peck Endowment)
Formerly in the collections of Mr. and Mrs. Albert Christian Revi, and Dr. and Mrs. Leonard S. Rakow

This is believed to be one of 40 blanks that were blown for Joseph Locke at Hodgetts, Richardson and Son. Most of them broke while the glass was being annealed.

BIBLIOGRAPHY: Whitehouse 2003, pp. 89–90, no. 1034.

37. Imitation of the Portland Vase

Germany, Munich, Franz Paul Zach (1820–1881), 1862
H. 28 cm, D. (rim) 11.4 cm
Blown, cased (translucent blue over colorless), engraved
The Corning Museum of Glass (92.3.79, purchased with funds from the Clara S. Peck Endowment)
Formerly in the collection of Dr. and Mrs. Leonard S. Rakow

Franz Paul Zach was a Bohemian engraver whose signed works include objects of glass and rock crystal. An imitation of the Portland Vase, engraved by Zach, was sent to the London world's fair of 1862. It may have been this imitation or a second copy of the vase, which is now in the Royal Albert Memorial Museum in Exeter, United Kingdom.

BIBLIOGRAPHY: Whitehouse 2003, pp. 85–86, no. 1031.

38. Portland Vase Blank

U.S., Corning, New York, William Gudenrath (b. 1950), 2007
H. 25.5 cm, W. 15 cm, Depth 11.5 cm
Blown, cased (dip-overlay method, opaque white over translucent blue)
The Corning Museum of Glass (2007.4.28)

This replica of the blank from which the Portland Vase is believed to have been carved was made at The Studio of The Corning Museum of Glass. It was produced by dipping a parison of blue glass into a pot of opaque white glass.

39. Reproduction of the Portland Vase

Germany, Josef Welzel (b. 1927), 1987
OH. 39.5 cm
Blown, cased, cut, ground, polished
Collection of Josef Welzel, Hadamar, Germany

After drawing the figural design on the amphora, Welzel removed the background with cutting wheels and abrasive powder. To enhance the three-dimensional effect, the contours were undercut, using the flat part of the wheel, which also smoothed the background. This is a gem-carving rather than glass-cutting technique. The artist, who believes that the Portland Vase probably had a cover, cast and cut a cobalt glass cover for his reproduction. The blank for this reproduction was supplied by the Christinenhütte, Schott, in Zwiesel, Germany.

BIBLIOGRAPHY: Welzel 1992.

40. The Great Tazza

England, Amblecote, Thomas Webb & Sons, George Woodall (1850–1925), about 1889
H. 38.9 cm
Blown (from two gathers), cased (opaque pink over opaque white over opaque green over opaque white over semiopaque deep green), acid-dipped, cameo-carved, engraved
The Corning Museum of Glass (92.2.8, bequest of Juliette K. Rakow)
Formerly in the collection of Dr. and Mrs. Leonard S. Rakow

This five-layered cameo glass tazza is a tour de force of cameo glass carving. The bowl and the pedestal were made separately and then attached with a brass screw. After unwanted glass had been removed by dipping the blank in acid, each of the layers was carved by a team of craftsmen directed by George Woodall. The design for the tazza was inspired by *Examples of Chinese Ornament* by Owen Jones, published in 1867. Production began in 1886, but the work was not completed until 1889.

BIBLIOGRAPHY: Whitehouse 1994, pp. 9, 33, and 61, fig. 28; Perry 2000, pp. 30 and 53.

41. Photograph of the Woodall Team with *The Great Tazza*

England, about 1895
H. 14.9 cm
Rakow Research Library, The Corning Museum of Glass (97796)

Depicted in this photograph are the members of the Woodall team, posed as if working on *The Great Tazza* and an amphora. The figures, from left to right, are: William Hill, Tom Farmer, Harry Davis, J. T. Fereday, Thomas Woodall, and George Woodall.

BIBLIOGRAPHY: *Cameo Glass* 1982, pp. 50–51, fig. 26.

42. Plaques with Portraits of Dr. and Mrs. Samuel Parkes Cadman

England, Amblecote, Thomas Webb & Sons, George Woodall (1850–1925), about 1895
Each: H. 15.7 cm, W. (max.) 11.3 cm
Cast, cased (opaque white over translucent reddish brown), acid-etched, cameo-carved
The Corning Museum of Glass (92.2.2A, B, gift of Juliette K. Rakow in memory of Leonard S. Rakow)
Formerly in the collection of Dr. and Mrs. Leonard S. Rakow

These plaques, which depict a highly successful evangelist and his wife, are among the most sensitively carved examples of English cameo glass. Dr. Cadman (1864–1936) was related to George Woodall through his mother, who was Woodall's sister-in-law. After arriving in the United States in 1890, Dr. Cadman served congregations in Yonkers, Millbrook, and Brooklyn, New York. He began a radio ministry in 1923, and this continued until his death. Cadman Plaza and Cadman Memorial Church in Brooklyn are named for him.

BIBLIOGRAPHY: Whitehouse 1994, pp. 41 and 61, fig. 36; Perry 2000, p. 74.

43. Plaque with Andromache

England, Amblecote, Thomas Webb & Sons, George Woodall (1850–1925), 1902
H. 31.2 cm, W. (max.) 22.9 cm
Cast, cased (opaque white over translucent reddish brown), etched, cameo-carved
The Corning Museum of Glass (89.2.9, gift of Juliette K. Rakow in memory of Leonard S. Rakow)
Formerly in the collection of Dr. and Mrs. Leonard S. Rakow

Andromache was the wife of Hector, son of King Priam of Troy. She is seen here framed by columns and an entablature, standing near a lighted brazier. In the distance, a city and a ship on the water are shown, demonstrating Woodall's extraordinary ability to create a feeling of perspective.

BIBLIOGRAPHY: Whitehouse 1994, pp. 51 and 62, fig. 47; Perry 2000, p. 90.

ANDROMACHE

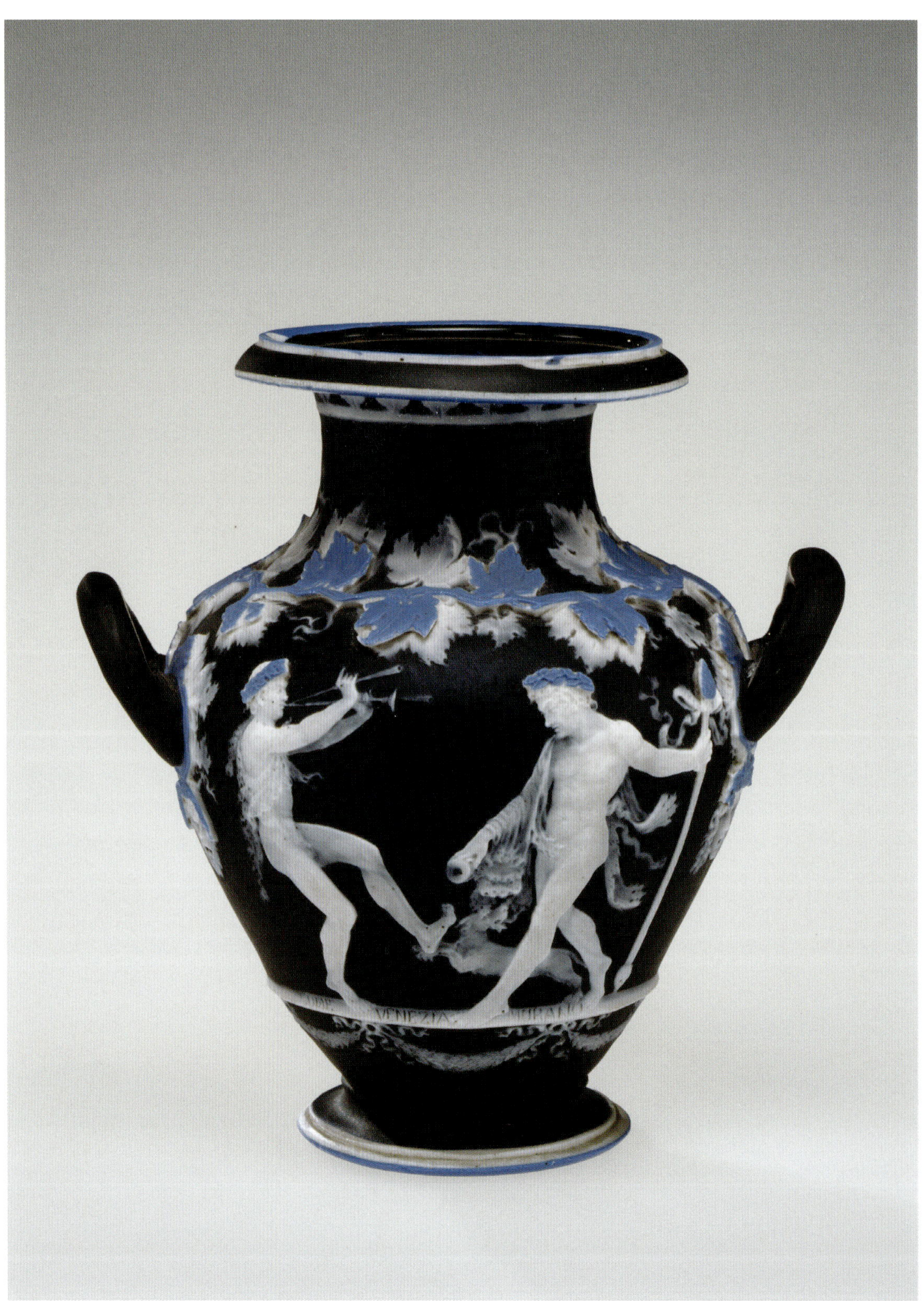
VENEZIA

44. Amphora with Dionysiac Scene

Italy, Venice, Compagnia di Venezia e Murano (C.V.M.),
Attilio Spaccarelli, 1891
H. 14.3 cm
Blown, cased (opaque light blue over opaque white over translucent deep blue), applied, cut
Collection of Martin Cohen, Watermill, New York (L.303.3.2000)

This vessel is unusual among 19th-century imitations of Roman cameo glass in that it has two superimposed overlays.

45. Bottle

Italy, Venice, Compagnia di Venezia e Murano (C.V.M.), 1885–1900
H. 16.7 cm
Blown, cased (opaque white over translucent blue), cold-worked
Yale University Art Gallery, New Haven, Connecticut (1955.6.46, bequest from Mrs. William H. Moore, 1955)
Formerly in the collections of Baron Wladimir von Greuneisen, Fahim Kouchakji, and Mrs. William H. Moore

This bottle is said to have been excavated at the Villa Albani (on the outskirts of Rome) by Carlo Marchione in 1760. The report is false. The bottle is an imitation of an ancient cameo glass vessel. The satyr was copied from a figure on the Roman marble krater known as the Borghese Vase, which is now in the Louvre, Paris.

BIBLIOGRAPHY: *Cameo Glass* 1982, p. 118, no. 87, and ill. p. 85.

46. Marquetry Vase with Flowers

France, Nancy, Cristallerie Emile Gallé, designed by Emile Gallé (1846–1904), about 1890–1900
H. 28.5 cm, D. (max.) 16.2 cm
Blown, cased, hot-applied, inlaid, acid-etched, cut, engraved; metal foil
The Corning Museum of Glass (56.3.38, gift of Astrid Varnay)
[Shown in Corning only.]

Emile Gallé, whose father was a glassmaker, set up his own glass factory in 1867. He designed cameo glasses of great originality, often with naturalistic ornament influenced by Japanese decoration. Gallé exhibited at the Paris world's fairs of 1878, 1889, and 1900.

C. Gold Glass
Roman Originals

47. Disch Cantharus

Roman Empire, late third to early fourth century A.D.
H. (surviving) 13.8 cm, D. (max.) 15.5 cm
Blown; decoration gilded and scratched; cage and handles applied
The Corning Museum of Glass (66.1.267)
Formerly in the collections of Charles Damien Disch, H. Hoffmann, and Giorgio Sangiorgi
[Shown in Corning only.]

This two-handled cup was found in Cologne, Germany, in 1864. It is decorated with gold foil that was applied to the outside of the cup and then carefully cut away so that only the figures of cupids playing among flowers remained. Unlike the gold glasses, however, the Disch Cantharus has no cover glass to protect the gold. Instead, the maker constructed a "poor man's cage cup" from trails of hot glass.

BIBLIOGRAPHY: Whitehouse 2001, pp. 275–277, no. 867.

48. Fragment with Greek Inscription

Roman Empire, third to fourth century A.D.
D. 7.8 cm
Blown (from two gathers); one parison decorated with flame-worked and gilded rods; second parison fused to decorated surface of first parison
The Corning Museum of Glass (66.1.31)

This is part of the base of a bowl. The Greek inscription (when seen from the inside) is "ƐΦƐCI / ZHC IC." In the second word, the letter *A* is missing. "ZHCAIC" (May you live!) is a common toast that is found on many drinking vessels. The first word may address a person named Ephesios or someone from the city of Ephesus.

BIBLIOGRAPHY: Whitehouse 2001, p. 243, no. 830.

49. Fragment with Pelorius

Roman Empire, fourth century A.D.
D. 6.2 cm
Parison for base blown; gold foil applied to upper surface and decorated with stylus; parison was reheated, and second parison was pressed against upper surface so that the two fused; parisons were then reworked to desired form
The Corning Museum of Glass (54.1.80)

The inscription, ".PELORI.PIE.ZESE[S.VIV]AS," means, "Pelorius, drink and may you live [for many years], may you live."

BIBLIOGRAPHY: Whitehouse 2001, p. 248, no. 840.

50. Fragment with Saints Peter and Paul

Roman Empire, fourth century A.D.
D. 9.2 cm
Made in the same manner as **49**
The Corning Museum of Glass (62.1.20)

Between the images of Saints Peter (*left*) and Paul stands a representation of Christ crowning the apostles with wreaths.

BIBLIOGRAPHY: Whitehouse 2001, pp. 248–249, no. 841.

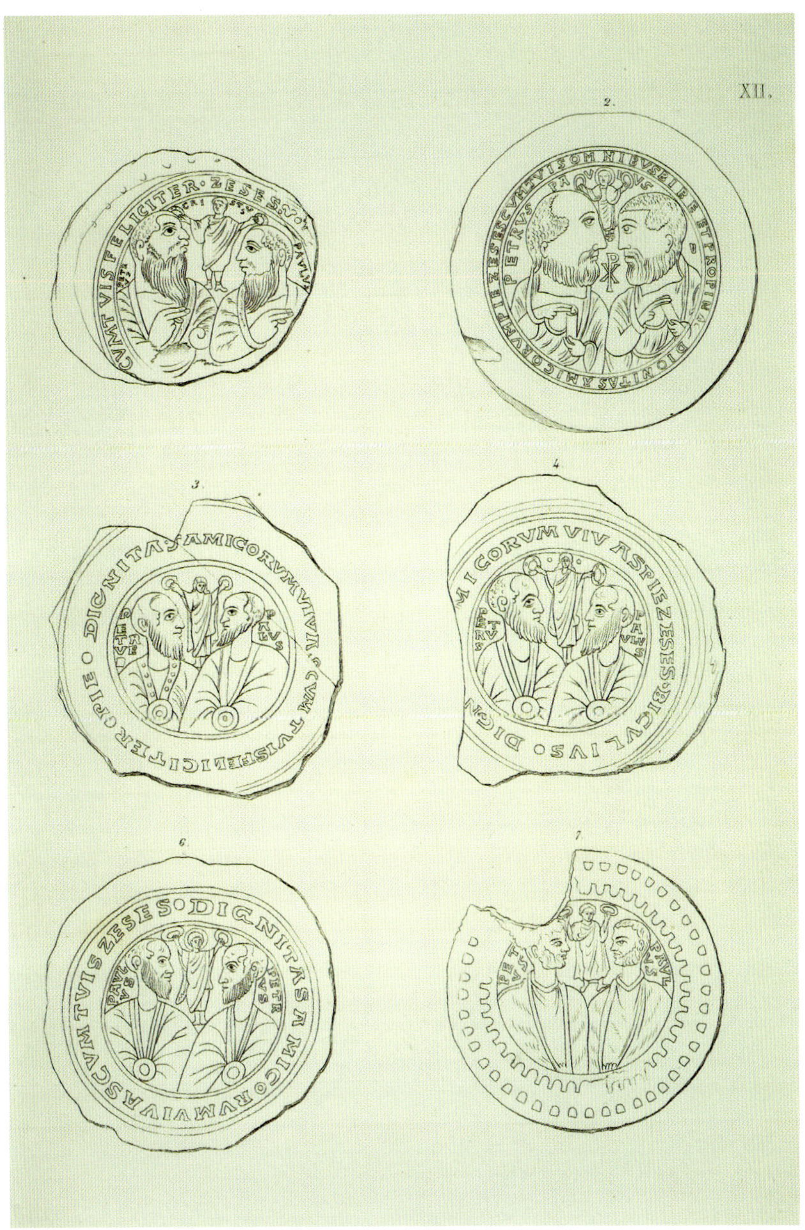

51. *Vetri ornati di figure in oro . . .*

Raffaele Garrucci (1812–1885), Vetri ornati di figure in oro trovati nei cimiteri dei cristiani primitivi di Roma/raccolti e spiegati da Raffaele Garrucci, *Rome: Tipografia Salviucci, 1858*
Rakow Research Library, The Corning Museum of Glass (51877)

Garrucci's publications of gold glasses found in the catacombs of Rome were the source of many of the designs used by Venetian glassmakers in the late 19th century.

Modern Imitations

52. Copy of the Disch Cantharus

Italy, Venice, Compagnia di Venezia e Murano (C.V.M.), or Germany, Ehrenfeld, Rheinische Glashütten A.G., late 19th century
H. 22.2 cm, D. (max.) 10.8 cm
Blown, gilded, applied
The Corning Museum of Glass (59.3.38)
Formerly in the collection of Ray Winfield Smith

This is one of several copies of **47**. It lacks the handles of the original, and its cage consists of seven zigzag trails instead of six. Copies of the Disch Cantharus were made in both Italy and Germany. All of the published examples are shown with handles. The slightly yellowish color of the glass of the Corning reproduction supports the view that it was made on Murano.

BIBLIOGRAPHY: Whitehouse 2003, p. 94, no. 1042.

53. Plaque

Italy, Venice, probably workshop of Francesco Toso Borella,
late 19th century
H. 2.6 cm, D. (max.) 16.8 cm
Blown (from two gathers), sandwiched gold-leaf decoration, ground
The Corning Museum of Glass (53.3.54)
Formerly in the collection of Mrs. Applewhaite-Abbott

This is probably a fragment from the base and foot of a large plate, bowl, or vase. It is attributed to Toso Borella (1846–1905), whose principal design sources were probably the monographs on gold glasses published by Raffaele Garrucci in 1858, 1864, and 1876. This example imitates a fourth-century gold glass in the Museo Sacro of the Vatican Library. Toso Borella's figures, however, do not follow the original closely, and one of the busts in the central medallion has a somewhat "Renaissance" appearance.

BIBLIOGRAPHY: Whitehouse 2003, pp. 94–95, no. 1043.

54. VASE

Italy, probably 1870–1890
H. 29.5 cm, D. (max.) 10.7 cm
Blown, applied, decorated with gold leaf
The Corning Museum of Glass (61.3.115)

The workshop of Francesco Toso Borella (1846–1905) may have produced this object, which is similar to gold glasses presented to the Museo Vetrario (now the Museo del Vetro), Murano, by his son. One of the monographs on gold glasses by Raffaele Garrucci, a probable source for the design, contains all four of the saints shown on the object.

BIBLIOGRAPHY: Whitehouse 2003, pp. 96–97, no. 1045.

55. Bowl

Italy, Venice, Francesco Toso Borella (1846–1905), about 1878
H. 9 cm, D. 16 cm
Blown (from two gathers), applied, decorated with gold leaf
Collection of Rainer Zietz, London

The bottom of this bowl is decorated with a scene of Christ raising Lazarus, or of Moses striking the rock. Both of these images are frequently found on fragments of Roman gold glasses that were placed in the catacombs. The scene here is ambiguous. Although the format of the picture suggests the raising of Lazarus, there is no tomb or wrapped body as is found in the other representations. In images of Moses striking the rock, water is always indicated on the other examples, but not here.

56. Dish

Italy, Venice, Francesco Toso Borella (1846–1905), about 1878
D. 22 cm
Blown (from two gathers), applied, decorated with gold leaf
Collection of Rainer Zietz, London

The scene on the bottom of this dish shows Christ and the miracle of the Wedding at Cana. The firm of Toso Borella, the Compagnia di Venezia e Murano (C.V.M.), and the Salviati company all made reproductions of early Christian gold glasses.

BELLICIA
FEDELISSIMA
VIRCO
INPACE
IIII X
CALENDAS
BENTURAS
SEPTEM
BRES
QUE VIXIT
ANNOS
XVIII

57. Plaque

Italy, Venice, late 19th century
D. 13.5 cm
Blown (from two gathers), applied, decorated with gold leaf
The J. Paul Getty Museum, Malibu, California (JPGM 2003.296)
Formerly in the collection of Erwin Oppenländer

This plaque is a forgery that reproduces a scene incised on a gravestone in the Vatican Museum. Unlike other modern reproductions, which are often embedded in the bodies of vessels, the edges of this object have been deliberately chipped in order to make it appear to be ancient. The Latin inscription identifies the praying figure as Bellicia.

BIBLIOGRAPHY: *Oppenländer Collection* 1974, p. 142, no. 400.

D. Mosaic Glass
Roman Originals

58. Gold-Band Cup

Roman Empire, late first century B.C. to early first century A.D.
H. 11.5 cm
Canes assembled and fused, then slumped over mold; rim, handles, and foot applied
The Metropolitan Museum of Art, New York (GR 91.1.2053, bequest of Edward C. Moore, 1891)
Formerly in the collection of Alessandro Castellani

This is the only known ancient example of a gold-band vessel of this shape. Following the death of the collector Alessandro Castellani in 1883, his collection was sold. The sale catalog described the cup as a "magnifique kanthare de la fabrique de Toscanella." *Toscanella* (modern Tuscania), an ancient Etruscan city, was a rich source of antiquities, and Castellani and other 19th-century collectors regarded mosaic glass as part of that culture.

BIBLIOGRAPHY: Page, Pilosi, and Wypyski 2001, pp. 129–130 and fig. 15; Picón and others 2007, pp. 335 and 482–483, no. 389.

59. Dish

Roman Empire, first century B.C. to first century A.D.
H. 2.1 cm, D. 16 cm
Assembled from slices of canes, cast; base-ring applied; rotary-polished
The J. Paul Getty Museum, Malibu, California (JPGM 85.AF.85)
Formerly in the collection of Ernst Kofler and Marthe Truniger

This object belongs to a group of remarkably homogeneous vessels that may have been made in Italy during the reigns of Emperors Augustus (27 B.C.–A.D. 14) and Tiberius (A.D. 14–37).

BIBLIOGRAPHY: *Kofler-Truniger Collection* 1964, p. 46, no. 459, pl. 36; *3000 Jahre Glaskunst* 1981, pp. 15, 63, and 160.

60. PATELLA CUP

Roman Empire, eastern Mediterranean, first century B.C. to first century A.D.
H. 4.1 cm, D. (rim) 9.6 cm
Mosaic glass technique, ground, polished
The Corning Museum of Glass (55.1.82)
Formerly in the collection of Ray Winfield Smith

Face canes were rarely embedded in bowls. Four cane slices with female busts are distributed evenly on the bottom of this cup. The object also features a checkerboard pattern of diamond-shaped canes that are arranged in groups of four to form large diamonds.

BIBLIOGRAPHY: Goldstein 1979, pp. 186–187, no. 497; *Glass of the Caesars* 1987, p. 43, no. 19; Bruhn 1995, pp. 11–13, figs. 11 and 12.

Modern Imitations

61. Cup

Italy, Venice, Compagnia di Venezia e Murano (C.V.M.), probably Vincenzo Moretti (1835–1901), 1878
H. 8.8 cm, D. (max.) 21.5 cm
Canes assembled and fused, then slumped over mold; handles and foot-ring applied
The Corning Museum of Glass (64.3.16)

This is one of four finished imitations of **58**. Barovier (1974, p. 116) stated that one of the reproductions was displayed at the 1878 world's fair in Paris. The bowl and the solid foot were cast in one piece.

BIBLIOGRAPHY: Goldstein 1979, p. 299, no. 914; Sarpellon 1995, pp. 105 and 183, fig. 793; Page, Pilosi, and Wypyski 2001, pp. 130–131, fig. 17, and p. 133.

62. Ribbon Glass Bowl

Italy, Venice, Compagnia di Venezia e Murano (C.V.M.), Vincenzo Moretti (1835–1901), about 1880
H. 6.2 cm, D. (rim) 11.2 cm
Canes assembled and fused, then slumped over mold; lathe-polished
The Corning Museum of Glass (50.3.76)
Formerly in the collection of George D. Macbeth

Although this object is derived from ancient ribbon glass bowls, its inclusion of characteristic face canes and one "VM" cane in the center identifies it as a product of the Compagnia di Venezia e Murano. In addition, the form is thoroughly modern. A hemispherical bowl is combined with a flared dish that has been inverted.

BIBLIOGRAPHY: Goldstein 1979, p. 297, no. 907; Sarpellon 1995, pp. 118 and 183, fig. 933.

63. Bowl

Italy, Venice, Compagnia di Venezia e Murano (C.V.M.),
Vincenzo Moretti (1835–1901), about 1880
H. 5.1 cm, D. (rim) 14.2 cm
Canes assembled and fused, then slumped over mold; lathe-polished
The Corning Museum of Glass (53.3.55)
Formerly in the collection of Mrs. Applewhaite-Abbott

In this shallow bowl, floral *murrine* are combined with slices of a spiral cane.

BIBLIOGRAPHY: Goldstein 1979, p. 296, no. 905; Page, Pilosi, and Wypyski 2001, pp. 119 and 121, fig. 5.

64. Dish

Italy, Venice, Compagnia di Venezia e Murano (C.V.M.), attributed to Vincenzo Moretti (1835–1901), about 1880
H. 2.7 cm, D. (rim) 11.7 cm
Canes assembled and fused, then slumped over mold; polished
The Corning Museum of Glass (76.3.42, gift of Carl Berkowitz and Derek Content)
Formerly in the collection of Ray Winfield Smith

Lotus blossoms and other stylized flowers are found in Vincenzo Moretti's samples of cane patterns. The design of this object is therefore attributed to him.

BIBLIOGRAPHY: Sarpellon 1995, pp. 117 and 183, fig. 922; Page, Pilosi, and Wypyski 2001, pp. 119–120, fig. 3.

65. Cup

Italy, Venice, The Venice and Murano Glass Company, about 1870–1880
H. 9.5 cm, D. (bowl) 13.8 cm
Canes assembled and fused, then slumped over mold; handles and foot applied
The Metropolitan Museum of Art, New York (ESDA 81.8.254, gift of James Jackson Jarves, 1881)
Formerly in the collection of James Jackson Jarves

This vessel is an unfinished copy of **58**. A recent X-radiograph (see bibliography) showed that the base-disk fused to the vessel incompletely. This indicates that, although the Venetian glassmakers were able to match the overall design and the colors of the ancient cup, they were less successful, in this instance, in duplicating the fabrication technique.

BIBLIOGRAPHY: Page, Pilosi, and Wypyski 2001, pp. 130–131, fig. 16, and p. 133, fig. 20.

66. Cup

Italy, Venice, Compagnia di Venezia e Murano (C.V.M.), about 1878
H. 9.2 cm, D. 14.2 cm
Canes assembled and fused, then slumped over mold; handles and foot applied
Smithsonian American Art Museum, Washington, D.C. (1929.8.147.27, gift of John Gellatly)

This is another copy of **58**. The design of the handles more closely resembles the ancient original.

BIBLIOGRAPHY: Page, Pilosi, and Wypyski 2001, pp. 130 and 132, fig. 18.

67. Cup

Italy, Venice, Compagnia di Venezia e Murano (C.V.M.), before 1888
H. 4.7 cm, D. 15.2 cm
Canes assembled and fused, then slumped over mold; rim, handles, and foot applied
MAK – Austrian Museum of Applied Arts/Contemporary Art, Vienna (G1 1812/1887)

Like the other reproductions of **58**, this vessel has a spiral cane rim. Its proportions, however, are more squat than those of the original and the other reproductions.

BIBLIOGRAPHY: Page, Pilosi, and Wypyski 2001, pp. 130 and 132, fig. 19.

68. Ribbed Bowl

Italy, Venice, The Venice and Murano Glass Company, about 1875–1900
H. 4.9 cm, D. 7.3 cm
Assembled from sections of canes, cast; ribs made of spirally twisted canes, applied
Yale University Art Gallery, New Haven, Connecticut (1955.6.39, bequest of Mrs. William H. Moore, 1955)

Although mosaic glass bowls and ribbed bowls were made in large quantities in the first centuries B.C. and A.D., this combination of a cast bowl and applied ribs was unknown.

BIBLIOGRAPHY: Matheson 1980, p. 141, no. A4.

69. Dish

Italy, Venice, Compagnia di Venezia e Murano (C.V.M.), Vincenzo Moretti (1835–1901), about 1878–1880
D. 11.7 cm
Assembled from sections of canes, cast
Museo del Vetro, Murano, Italy (class VI, no. 1785)
[Shown in Corning only.]

This dish replicates an ancient piece, found at Pompeii, that is now in the Museo Archeologico Nazionale, Naples. In 1879, Vincenzo Moretti traveled to Naples to study ancient glass in the museum for possible reproduction.

70. DISH

Italy, Venice, Salviati Dott. Antonio, Giovanni Barovier (1839–1908), 1881
D. 22.5 cm
Assembled from sections of canes, cast
Museo del Vetro, Murano, Italy (class VI, no. 1794)
[Shown in Corning only.]

Like Vincenzo Moretti, Giovanni Barovier studied ancient glass in order to reproduce it in his own work. The design of this vessel is based on a sketch made by Barovier of an ancient glass plaque in the collection of The British Museum, London (**76**).

BIBLIOGRAPHY: Sarpellon 1995, pp. 139 and 185, fig. 982.

71. Dish

Italy, Venice, Compagnia di Venezia e Murano (C.V.M.), Vincenzo Moretti (1835–1901), about 1880
D. 34.7 cm
Assembled from sections of canes, cast
Museo del Vetro, Murano, Italy (class VI, no. 1782)
[Shown in Corning only.]

This dish is nearly identical to one in the Musée des Arts Décoratifs in Paris. Incorporated into the pattern is a signature cane with the superimposed initials "VM."

BIBLIOGRAPHY: Sarpellon 1995, pp. 103 and 182, figs. 789 and 790.

72. Dish

Italy, Venice, Vincenzo Moretti (1835–1901), 1879–1883
D. 29.2 cm
Assembled from sections of canes, cast
Musée des Arts Décoratifs, Paris (A8 achat E.U. 1878)

This dish was displayed at the Paris world's fair of 1878, and it was purchased by the museum in that same year. A nearly identical dish is in the Museo del Vetro, Murano. The deep yellow foliated *murrine* on the example in the Paris museum were extremely difficult to make. This dish, unlike its near replica on Murano, does not contain Moretti's signature cane.

BIBLIOGRAPHY: Sarpellon 1995, p. 102.

73. VASE

Italy, Venice, The Venice and Murano Glass Company, 1871–1872
H. 11.7 cm, W. 10 cm
Blown, picked-up mosaic cane slices, marvered, inflated; handles applied
Victoria and Albert Museum, Ceramics and Glass Collection, London (1188-1873)

This vase was purchased by the museum from Salviati's company in 1873. It was manufactured by applying slices of a yellow cane, encircled by a dark red band surrounded by a green ring containing eight yellow dots, to a ground of green blown glass. The slices were fused to the green glass base, allowing the vessel to be fashioned by further inflation and manipulation.

BIBLIOGRAPHY: *Reflections of Venice* 1986, no. 34; *Miniature di vetro* 1990, pp. 96–97 and 187; Sarpellon 1995, pp. 93–94 and 182, fig. 701.

74. Bowl

Perhaps Italy, Venice, possibly Compagnia di Venezia e Murano (C.V.M.), 1880s
Canes fused, slumped over form, ground, polished
D. 15.7 cm
The J. Paul Getty Museum, Malibu, California (JPGM 2003.254)
Formerly in the collection of Erwin Oppenländer

It is difficult to distinguish this hemispherical bowl from the ancient originals it replicates. However, scientific analysis has determined that the glass used to create the vessel contains elements that were not used in antiquity. An analysis by the Getty Conservation Institute revealed that all of the colors of this bowl were made with glass containing 30- to 40-percent lead oxide. According to the institute's Dr. Marc Walton, "While lead is sometimes associated with colorants (such as in lead-tin yellow), lead at the levels in this bowl are inconsistent with Hellenistic and Roman glassmaking practice, in which soda was used as the flux." The object, he says, can therefore "be dated to a more modern period."

BIBLIOGRAPHY: *Oppenländer Collection* 1974, p. 122, no. 327.

75. Bowl

U.K., Quarley, Hampshire, Mark Taylor and David Hill, about 2003
D. 14.8 cm
Mosaic glass canes, fused, slumped
Private collection

This is a replica of a first-century A.D. mosaic glass bowl that is similar to a bowl found at Radnage, Buckinghamshire, England, which is now in The British Museum, London (PRB 1923.6-5.1). Because the bowl is such a close imitation of a Roman original, the makers have included one cane slice that indicates its modern source.

76. Sketch of Glass Plaque Fragments in The British Museum

Italy, Venice, Giovanni Barovier (1839–1908), 1866–1870
H. 14 cm, W. 19 cm
Collection of Marino Barovier, Venice
Formerly in the collections of Benvenuto Barovier and Anna Barovier

This sketch preserves images of ancient glass plaques in the collection of The British Museum, London. Barovier used the design of the fragmentary plaque on the left to create a mosaic dish.

BIBLIOGRAPHY: Sarpellon 1995, pp. 138–139 and 185, fig. 981.

Roman Cane Slices

77. Cane Slice with Head of Satyr

Roman Empire, first century B.C. to first century A.D.
L. 2.8 cm, W. (max.) 1.3 cm
Groups of canes assembled and fused to form composite bar, which was then cut into slices
The Corning Museum of Glass (59.1.95)
Formerly in the collection of Ray Winfield Smith

The most elaborate Hellenistic canes are those with faces and other decorative imagery. The slices were cut from complex bars made of composite parts. They are often attributed to Alexandrian workshops because of their Egyptian motifs, but many of them may have come from Rome. Halves of faces were used, as in this instance, to form complete, symmetrical faces by combining two slices from the same bar, one of which was reversed.

BIBLIOGRAPHY: Goldstein 1979, p. 237, no. 689; Bruhn 1995, p. 11, fig. 9.

78. Cane Slice with Theatrical Mask

Roman Empire, first century B.C. to first century A.D.
H. 3.4 cm
Groups of canes assembled and fused to form composite bar, which was then cut into slices
The J. Paul Getty Museum, Malibu, California (JPGM 2004.28)
Formerly in the collection of Erwin Oppenländer

As with the other cane slices displayed here, a complete face was created by placing identical cane slices side by side. This cane depicts a theatrical mask of a female character wearing an elaborate wig.

BIBLIOGRAPHY: *Oppenländer Collection* 1974, pp. 121 (color pl.) and 126, no. 335c.

Modern Imitations

79. Cane Slices, *Aegyptica Antika*

U.S., McKinleyville, California, Dinah Hulet (b. 1949), 2006
Tallest: H. 3.4 cm
Groups of canes assembled and fused to form composite bar, which was then cut into slices
Collection of the artist

In creating her replicas of ancient Roman and Egyptian canes, Dinah Hulet carefully constructs the scenes element by element, and fuses these elements together to create the final image. Using an open flame, she heats monochrome canes, and using simple tools, she shapes them to the desired effect. She adds canes of additional colors, reheating and shaping them with tools until the design is created. She then uses a block to make the cane square in profile. After further reheating, she stretches the cane to miniaturize the design. The resulting cane can then be assembled with others of the same design, or with different designs, by securing them together with lengths of copper wire and heating them until they fuse. When all of the selected elements have been fused together, they are reheated and stretched again to further miniaturize the final design.

This process is illustrated at http://huletglass.com/x/AIHV/GlassCanes1.htm.

BIBLIOGRAPHY: *Good Things/Small Packages* 2006, p. 29.

E. Cage Cups
Roman Originals

80. Rothschild Lycurgus Cup

Roman Empire, fourth century A.D.
H. 16.5 cm, D. (rim) 13.2 cm
Blown (possibly mold-blown), cold-worked
The British Museum, London (MLA 1958.12-.2.1)

This is one of the most remarkable late Roman glass objects. The glass is dichroic: it appears to be one color (green) in reflected light and a different color (red) when light shines through it. The scene depicts the myth of Lycurgus, a Thracian king who intruded upon the secret rituals of Dionysus and his followers. The king was punished when one of the maenads, Ambrosia, was transformed into a vine, which strangled him.

BIBLIOGRAPHY: *Glass of the Caesars* 1987, pp. 245–249, no. 139.

81. Cage Cup

Roman Empire, fourth century A.D.
H. 7.4 cm, D. (max.) 12.2 cm
Blown or cast, wheel-cut, polished
The Corning Museum of Glass (87.1.1, purchased with funds from the Arthur Rubloff Residuary Trust)

The metal collar with the three perforated flanges indicates that this object was meant to be suspended. While the function of Roman hanging bowls can only be inferred, descriptions and illustrations in contemporary manuscripts show that similar objects served as lamps in the Byzantine period. Therefore, it is reasonable to suppose that this cage cup was a hanging lamp.

BIBLIOGRAPHY: Whitehouse 1997, pp. 283–285, no. 478.

82. Cage Cup

Roman Empire, fourth century A.D.
H. 9.5 cm, D. 8.9 cm
Blown or cast, wheel-cut, polished
Kunsthistorisches Museum, Vienna (X1a 186)
Formerly in the collection of Prince Johann Sigismund Khevenhüller-Metsch

This cage cup was found in Daruvar, Croatia, in 1785. The incomplete Latin inscription, "...]FAVENTIB[VS ...," means "to those who favor" (that is, "to our protectors").

BIBLIOGRAPHY: Harden and Toynbee 1959, no. B5; Weinberg 1964, pp. 53–54, fig. 15; Cermanović-Kuzmanović 1979.

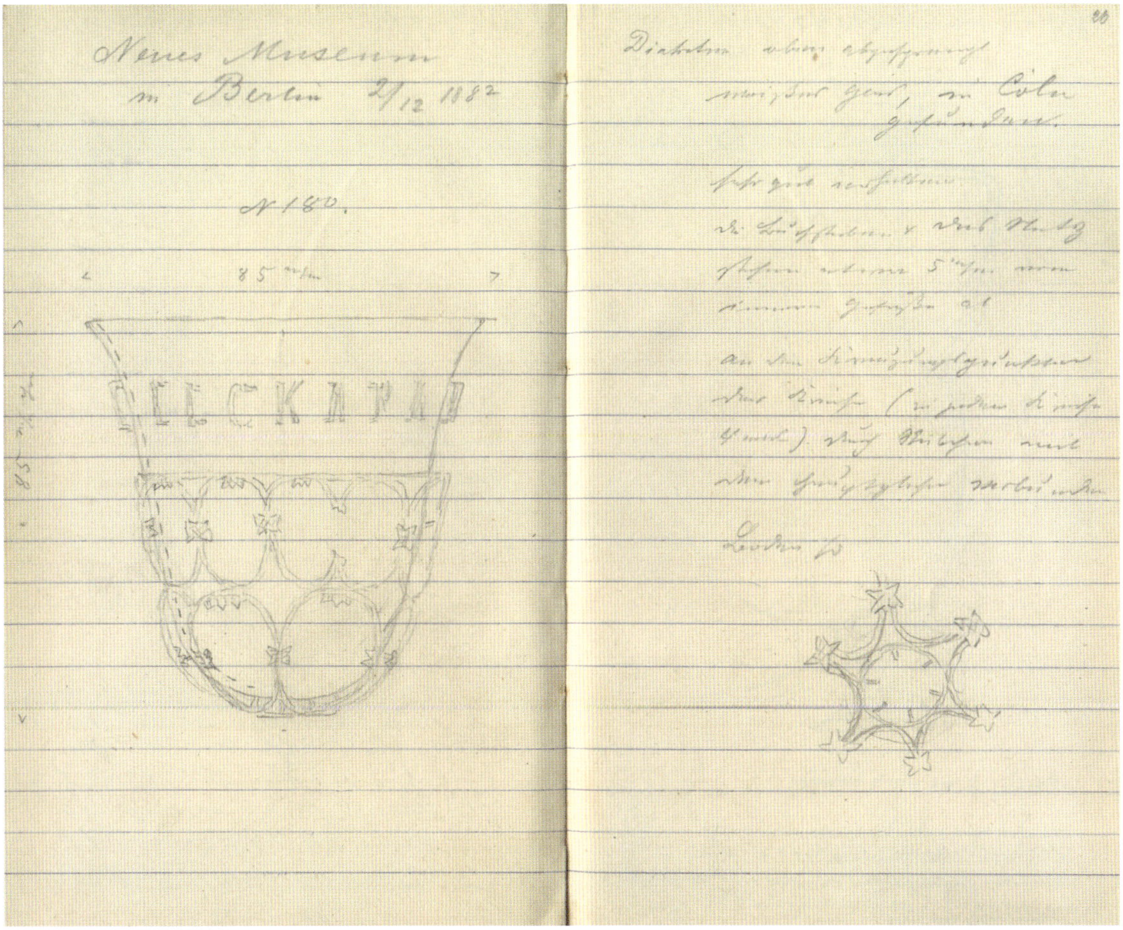

83. Sketch of Cage Cup in Berlin

Germany, Ehrenfeld, Rheinische Glashütten A.G., Oskar Rauter, 1882
16.5 cm x 10.1 cm
Museum Kunst Palast Düsseldorf, Glasmuseum Hentrich (Nachlass Rauter, no. 13, bequest of Caroline Rauter)

Oskar Rauter, head of the Rheinische Glashütten, traveled widely in Europe and the eastern United States in order to sketch and take notes on various ancient glass vessels that he wanted to reproduce. This sketchbook, labeled "Berlin 1882," documents the vessels he saw there, including this Roman cage cup, which no longer exists.

BIBLIOGRAPHY: Zobel-Klein 2003a, pp. 163–166 and fig. 5.

Modern Imitations

84. Cage Cup

Hungary, Zlatnó, glassworks of J. György Zahn, designed by Leó Valentin Pantocsek (1812–1893), about 1867
H. 10.2 cm
Blown, applied, cut
Iparművészeti Múzeum (Museum of Applied Arts), Budapest (23.315)
Formerly in the collection of Vince Wartha

This is not a copy of any known cage cup. However, the design was inspired by Roman cage cups, such as the Trivulzio Cage Cup, which was found in 1675; the Daruvar cage cup (**82**), which was found in 1785; and the cage cups found in Cologne in 1844 (see page 27).

85. Imitation of the Strasbourg Cage Cup

Italy, Venice, Compagnia di Venezia e Murano (C.V.M.), 1878
H. 32 cm
Blown, applied (deep green and purple over colorless)
Museo del Vetro, Murano, Italy (class VI, no. 1769)
[Shown in Corning only.]

This is an imitation of a cage cup discovered at Strasbourg, France, in 1825 and destroyed during the Franco-Prussian War in 1870. The inscription, which was incomplete on the broken original, refers to Emperor Maximian (r. A.D. 286–310). The imitation is furnished with a hollow foot, which almost certainly was not part of the original object.

BIBLIOGRAPHY: *Mille anni* 1982, p. 222, no. 412.

86. Cage Cup

Italy, Venice, Salviati and Company, 1890–1913
H. 23.5 cm, D. 18.3 cm
Blown; fish and cage rings made separately and applied
Iris and B. Gerald Cantor Center for Visual Arts at Stanford University, Stanford, California (11270, gift of Maurizio Camerino and Silvio Salviati)

Although the shape is entirely different, the decoration of this beaker recalls the layout of the ornament on a bucket-shaped cage cup in the Treasury of San Marco, Venice. Like the ancient example, this vessel has a cage network covering the bottom, with figural decoration at the top. A hunting scene decorates the San Marco example. A row of slanting fish appears on the upper portion of the modern vessel. Below it are three horizontal rows of glass rings held in place by applied trails in a pattern resembling the ancient circular patterning. This vessel and many other works from the Salviati and Company catalog were donated to the Stanford Art Gallery by Maurizio Camerino and Silvio Salviati.

BIBLIOGRAPHY: Osborne 2002, p. 51, no. 5.

87. "DIATRETA" VASE

U.S., Corning, New York, Steuben Glass Inc., Frederick Carder (1863–1963), 1958
H. 20.6 cm, D. (max.) 16.5 cm
Cast (lost wax technique)
The Corning Museum of Glass (59.4.356, gift of Corning Glass Works)

Frederick Carder was in his 90s when he produced a series of variations on the theme of cage cups. Paul Hollister, who wrote extensively on the history of glass, commented, "It is almost inconceivable that anyone could attempt to cast a complete cage cup in a single operation by *cire perdue* [lost wax casting]; Carder did" (*Brilliance in Glass* 1993, p. 8).

BIBLIOGRAPHY: *Brilliance in Glass* 1993, p. 25.

88. Reproduction of the Daruvar Cage Cup

Germany, Munich, Fritz W. Schäfer (b. 1943), 1964
H. 9.8 cm, D. (rim) 9.1 cm
Blown, ground, polished
Collection of Fritz W. Schäfer, Ratingen, Germany

Fritz W. Schäfer, who received a diploma in glass design from the Akademie der Bildenden Künste (Academy of Fine Arts) in Munich, is a designer in Ratingen and Munich, Germany. He has presented lectures on cage cups at international congresses on glass and design in Venice, London, and Munich. His reproduction of **82** has been shown at the Deutsches Museum, Munich; The British Museum, London; and The Corning Museum of Glass.

BIBLIOGRAPHY: Schäfer 1968.

89. Reproduction of the Rothschild Lycurgus Cup

Germany, Josef Welzel (b. 1927), 1970
H. 17.5 cm
Blown, ground, cut, polished
Collection of Josef Welzel, Hadamar, Germany

For this reproduction, the Wiesenthal glasshouse in Schwäbisch Gmünd provided a blank that was based on the composition of **80** as determined at The British Museum. The glass shows a similar ruby color in transmitted light, but it does not reproduce the opaque green appearance of the original in reflected light. One seated figure and the panther are cut in the same manner as the sea creatures on the cage cup from Szekszárd. The bodies of the figures were hollowed out from the inside of the cup. The reproduction is slightly taller than the original because a missing part of the base of the ancient vessel has been reconstructed.

BIBLIOGRAPHY: Welzel 1994, pp. 21–24.

90. Reproduction of the Köln-Braunsfeld Cage Cup

Germany, Josef Welzel (b. 1927), 1971
H. 12 cm
Blown, applied, ground, cut, polished
Collection of Josef Welzel, Hadamar, Germany

The original cage cup was found in a grave in the family cemetery at a Roman country house on the outskirts of Cologne, Germany, in 1960. It was made in the first half of the fourth century A.D. The blank for this reproduction had to be ordered from Argentina in 1970 because there was no glassmaker in Germany who could produce a glass with three overlays at that time. The inner vessel was shaped, smoothed, and polished underneath the network, and the size of the engraving wheels had to be adapted accordingly.

BIBLIOGRAPHY: Welzel 1994, pp. 25–42.

91. Stages in the Making of a Cage Cup

U.K., Edinburgh, George D. Scott (1946–2001), 1988–1989
Tallest: H. 14.4 cm, D. (rim) 11.9 cm
Blown, ground, cut, polished
The Corning Museum of Glass (89.2.22, gift of Juliette K. Rakow in memory of Leonard S. Rakow)

Inspired by illustrations in the catalog that accompanied the exhibition "Glass of the Caesars" in 1987–1988 (*Glass of the Caesars* 1987), George D. Scott made several replicas of late Roman cage cups.

BIBLIOGRAPHY: Scott 1991.

F. Iridescence
Ancient Vessels with Unintended Iridescence

92. Head Flask

Roman Empire, fourth to fifth century A.D.
H. 17.2 cm, W. 8 cm
Mold-blown; foot and handle applied
The J. Paul Getty Museum, Malibu, California (JPGM 85.AF.320)
Formerly in the collection of Ernst Kofler and Marthe Truniger

The iridescent surface of this object was caused by interference effects of light reflected from several layers of weathering. The weathering was caused by chemical reactions between the glass and its environment.

BIBLIOGRAPHY: *3000 Jahre Glaskunst* 1981, pp. 5 and 84.

93. Flask with Geometric Pattern

Eastern Roman Empire, third to fourth century A.D.
H. 8.2 cm
Mold-blown
The J. Paul Getty Museum, Malibu, California (JPGM 2003.336)
Formerly in the collection of Erwin Oppenländer

The entire surface of this small sprinkler flask is covered with iridescence, making it difficult to discern the original blue-green color.

BIBLIOGRAPHY: *Oppenländer Collection* 1974, pp. 168 (color pl.) and 175, no. 483.

94. Bottle

Islamic, probably Middle East, about ninth century A.D.
H. 15.3 cm
Blown
The J. Paul Getty Museum, Malibu, California (JPGM 78.AF.23)
Formerly in the collection of H. Leonard Simmons

This simple form was made in several parts of the Islamic world, perhaps over an extended period. Since that time, its surface has changed to an iridescent blue-green.

BIBLIOGRAPHY: *Arts of Fire* 2004, pp. 78–79, pl. 2.

95. Flagon or Amphora

Eastern Roman Empire, fourth to fifth century A.D.
H. (restored) 31 cm, D. (max.) 9.4 cm
Body partly inflated in dip mold; trails and handle(s) applied
The Corning Museum of Glass (65.1.40)

The closest parallels for this object are amphoras, but there is no trace of a second handle, and it may well have been a flagon. The use of a modern eyedropper to restore the base of the object was detected by radiography.

BIBLIOGRAPHY: Whitehouse 2001, pp. 185–186, no. 730.

Modern Vessels with Intentional Iridescence

96. Goblet

England, London, James Powell & Sons, Whitefriars, about 1900
H. 25.9 cm, D. (rim) 17 cm
Blown, fumed
The Corning Museum of Glass (85.2.13)

The Whitefriars glasshouse was established in the late 17th century. During the 19th century, it acquired a reputation for making stained glass windows. Among its designers were the Pre-Raphaelites Edward Burne-Jones, Philip Webb, and Ford Madox Brown. By the end of the 19th century, Whitefriars was also producing fine tableware.

97. Favrile Bowl

U.S., Corona, New York, Tiffany Studios, Louis Comfort Tiffany (1848–1933), about 1900–1920
H. 7.6 cm, D. (rim) 20.1 cm
Mold-blown, iridized
The Corning Museum of Glass (63.4.128, gift of Fletcher Ford and Mrs. Sally Recker in memory of Lola Kincaid Ford)

The iridescent finish on the Favrile glass of Louis Comfort Tiffany was meant to imitate the weathering on ancient Roman glasses that had been buried. The colors were produced by spraying the hot surface of the glass with metallic salts. Tiffany patented Favrile in 1894.

98. Vase with Reserve Pattern

U.S., Corning, New York, Frederick Carder (1863–1963), 1913–1918
H. 31.3 cm, D. (max.) 29.4 cm
Blown, iridized, etched
Rockwell Museum of Western Art, Corning, New York (82.4.240F, bequeathed by Frank and Mary Elizabeth Reifschlager). Lent to The Corning Museum of Glass (L.1262.4.2001)

Despite the appearance of the decoration in reflected light, this vase is made of deep blue glass. The decoration was etched through the iridescent film, which Carder named Blue Aurene.

99. Jar

Hungary, Zlatnó, glassworks of J. György Zahn, Leó Valentin Pantocsek (1812–1893), about 1860s
H. 17 cm, D. (max.) 15 cm
Blown, iridized
Iparművészeti Múzeum (Museum of Applied Arts), Budapest (23.314)
Formerly in the collection of Vince Wartha

Iridized glass was inspired by efforts to reproduce the colorful effect of weathering on ancient glasses from archeological excavations. The Hungarian chemist Leó Valentin Pantocsek discovered the technique of iridizing glass at the Zlatnó factory in 1856. This process was adopted by Louis Comfort Tiffany in the United States and by the glasshouse of Johann Loetz Witwe in Bohemia. These makers, however, did not specialize in the imitation of ancient glasses. Instead, they used the technique to create Art Nouveau glass.

BIBLIOGRAPHY: Varga 2000, p. 119, no. 10.

100. Bottle with Two Handles

Hungary, Zlatnó, glassworks of J. György Zahn, Leó Valentin Pantocsek (1812–1893), about 1860s
H. 30.5 cm
Blown, applied, iridized
Iparművészeti Múzeum (Museum of Applied Arts), Budapest (23.312)
Formerly in the collection of Vince Wartha

The form of this object is reminiscent of bottles made in the Roman Empire in the third and fourth centuries A.D.

BIBLIOGRAPHY: Varga 2000, p. 123, no. 22.

101. Vase with Trailed Decoration

Bohemia, Klášterský Mlýn (Klostermühle), Johann Loetz Witwe, about 1900–1910
H. 22.7 cm, D. (rim) 13 cm
Blown, trailed
The Corning Museum of Glass (61.3.119, gift of T. B. Buchholz)

Founded by Johann Loetz in 1836, the factory was taken over by his widow, Susanna, in 1852. She renamed the firm Johann Loetz Witwe (widow). The most successful years were 1879–1908, when the factory was directed by Max Ritter von Spaun, the founder's grandson.

G. Blown and Mold-Blown Objects
Roman Originals

102. Fish Flask

Roman Empire, Cologne, first half of the third century A.D.
L. 19.8 cm
Blown, pinched, applied
Römisch-Germanisches Museum, Cologne (RGM 234)

This perfume flask is in the shape of a swimming fish. Its contents would have been visible through the colorless glass of its body. The flask was found in Cologne. Other examples of this type have been found on Cyprus.

BIBLIOGRAPHY: Doppelfeld 1966, p. 50+; Schäfke 1979, p. 29, fig. 34.

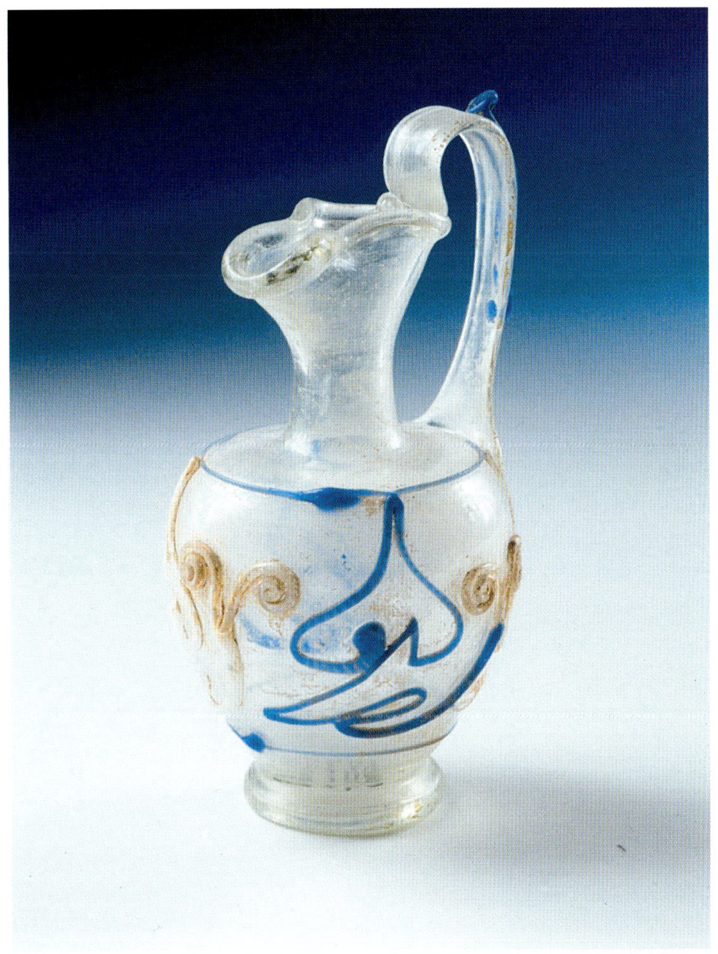

103. Jug with Trails

Roman Empire, third century A.D.
H. 12.8 cm
Blown; handle applied
Römisch-Germanisches Museum, Cologne (RGM 69.72.5)

This jug was found in Cologne, together with a handled dish. Such pairs of objects have been uncovered frequently, and finds in the Rhineland suggest that they were made in large quantities. Their shape and method of production are quite similar, and most of them are decorated with snake-thread trails. Jug-and-dish sets in this form and size appear to have been made only during the third century.

BIBLIOGRAPHY: *3000 Jahre Glaskunst* 1981, p. 110, nos. 431 and 432; *Glass of the Caesars* 1987, p. 128, no. 58.

104. Jug with Interior Jug

Roman Empire, Cologne, about A.D. 200
H. 31.5 cm
Smaller vessel blown, with applied trail and handle; parison of larger vessel blown and opened; smaller vessel inserted; larger vessel then blown to final form, with trail and handle applied
Römisch-Germanisches Museum, Cologne (RGM N 50)
Formerly in the Niessen and Merkens Collections

This vessel, which was found in Remagen, Germany, is remarkable for its construction of a vessel within a vessel. Because of its complex manufacture, it is not surprising that Oskar Rauter selected it for reproduction.

BIBLIOGRAPHY: La Baume 1964, p. 57+ and 61, pl. 49; Zobel-Klein 2003b, pp. 189–191 and fig. 13.

105. Scallop Amphora

Roman Empire, Cologne, about A.D. 300
H. 19 cm
Mold-blown; foot and handles applied
Römisch-Germanisches Museum, Cologne (RGM 529)

Ancient glassmakers took delight in imitating nature by creating vessels either with molds from actual examples or by fashioning them freehand. This flask is shaped like a scallop, with an added foot and applied handles. It was found in Cologne in 1893.

BIBLIOGRAPHY: La Baume 1964, p. 175, fig. 163; Doppelfeld 1966, p. 45+, pl. 51.

106. Snake-Thread Vessel

Roman Empire, late second to third century A.D.
H. 19.5 cm, D. 9.2 cm
Blown; foot and trails applied
The British Museum, London (GR 1984.7-16.1)

This object is said to have been found in Koblenz, Germany. It was acquired by The British Museum at auction in London in 1982. Numerous examples of the same type have been found in Cologne.

BIBLIOGRAPHY: *Glass of the Caesars* 1987, p. 132, no. 61.

107. Mythological Beaker

Roman Empire, first century A.D.
H. 12.7 cm, D. (rim) 6.4 cm
Mold-blown
The British Museum, London (GR 1878.10-20.1)

This object was found at the ancient site of Cyzicus, Turkey. The vessel was inflated in a five-part mold. To date, no modern glassmaker has been able to successfully reproduce the multiple-panel ancient molds, and no examples have survived from antiquity to shed light on their means of manufacture.

BIBLIOGRAPHY: Wight 1994, p. 29.

108. Leaf Beaker

Roman Empire, first century A.D.
H. 7.3 cm, D. 6.3 cm
Mold-blown
The J. Paul Getty Museum, Malibu, California (JPGM 85.AF.91)

This small drinking cup was inflated in a three-part mold using two side panels atop a separate base. The moldmaker skillfully concealed his seams in the stems of the small plants.

BIBLIOGRAPHY: Wight 2000.

109. *Preis-Courant der Rheinischen Glashütten-Actien-Gesellschaft . . .*

Rheinische Glashütten-Actien-Gesellschaft, Ehrenfeld, Germany, Preis-Courant der Rheinischen Glashütten-Actien-Gesellschaft in Ehrenfeld bei Köln (Rheinpreussen): Abtheilung für Kunst-Erzeugnisse (Gegenstände in den älteren Stylen), *Cologne: J. B. Heimann & Zimmermann, 1886*
Rakow Research Library, The Corning Museum of Glass (55370)

The Rheinische Glashütten made decorative and useful glasses in a variety of historical styles, including ancient Roman and Renaissance Venetian. The company issued two catalogs of historicizing glass, in 1881 and 1886.

BIBLIOGRAPHY: Schäfke 1979 (reprint, with introduction).

Modern Imitations

110. Reproduction of Jug with Trails

Germany, Ehrenfeld, Rheinische Glashütten A.G., 1910
H. 9.8 cm
Blown; foot and trails applied
Römisch-Germanisches Museum, Cologne (RGM 23.397)

This vessel reproduces an ancient vase that was found in Cologne and is now in the Rheinisches Landesmuseum Bonn. There are numerous ancient examples with this shape and decoration, attesting to their popularity in antiquity.

BIBLIOGRAPHY: Zobel-Klein 2003b, p. 191, fig. 14.

111. Reproduction of Jug with Interior Jug

Germany, Ehrenfeld, Rheinische Glashütten A.G., late 19th century
H. 31 cm
Smaller vessel blown, with applied trail and handle; parison of larger vessel blown and opened; smaller vessel inserted; larger vessel then blown to final form, with trail and handle applied
Römisch-Germanisches Museum, Cologne (RGM zu N 50)
Formerly in the Niessen Collection

Like the ancient object that inspired it (**104**), this vessel was formerly in the collection of Carl Anton Niessen, British consul in Cologne. Its complicated manufacturing techniques led to its selection for reproduction by the Rheinische Glashütten. The interior jug would have made it difficult for the vessel to serve as anything but a showpiece.

BIBLIOGRAPHY: Zobel-Klein 2003b, pp. 189–191 and fig. 14.

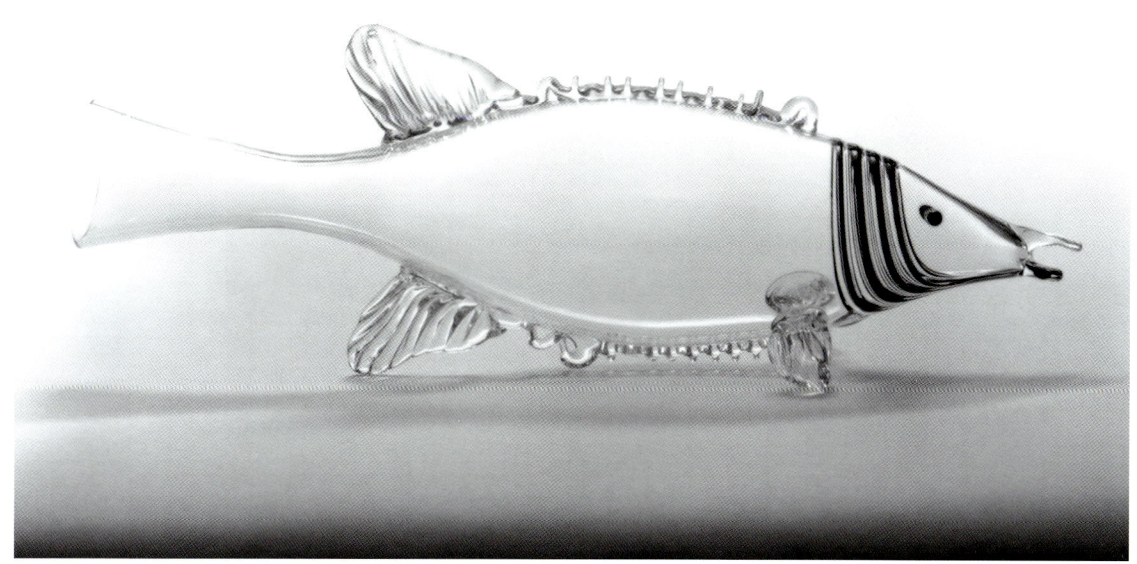

112. Reproduction of Fish Flask

Germany, Ehrenfeld, Rheinische Glashütten A.G.,
Oskar Rauter, 1886
H. 8.5 cm
Blown, pinched; applied trails
Kölnisches Stadtmuseum, Cologne (1926/566)

Reproductions of ancient vessels manufactured in Cologne included containers with whimsical shapes, such as this flask in the form of a fish. The ancient models (including **102**) were selected to highlight the technical skill of the glassmaker who was responsible for their manufacture.

BIBLIOGRAPHY: Schäfke 1979, p. 29, fig. 33.

113. Reproduction of Mythological Beaker

U.K., Quarley, Hampshire, Mark Taylor and David Hill, 1998
H. 12.8 cm, D. (rim) 6.7 cm
Mold-blown
Private collection

In their efforts to reproduce ancient vessels (such as **107**), Taylor and Hill use plaster for their molds. In doing so, they are able to achieve precise designs that are startling replicas of the ancient originals.

BIBLIOGRAPHY: www.romanglassmakers.co.uk/galbeak.htm.

114. Reproduction of Leaf Beaker

U.K., Quarley, Hampshire, Mark Taylor and David Hill, 2004
H. 8.5 cm, D. (rim) 6.4 cm
Mold-blown
Private collection

Exterior molds were taken from an ancient leaf beaker like **108** in order to replicate its pattern in plaster.

Bibliography: www.romanglassmakers.co.uk/galbeak.htm.

Bibliography

Most works are cited by author(s) and date (e.g., Northwood 1924). When the same author(s) published more than one work in a single year, the works are distinguished by lowercase letters immediately after the date (e.g., Painter and Whitehouse 1990a, b, c). Exhibition catalogs are cited by name and date (e.g., *Arts of Fire* 2004). Catalogs (including sale catalogs) of well-known private collections are cited by owner's name and date (e.g., *Beinecke Collection* 1965). Entries beginning with a cardinal or ordinal number, expressed either as a numeral or spelled out, will be found after the alphabetical entries, arranged numerically.

The following abbreviations are used in the bibliography and in the text:

A. Names of Publications

AnnAIHV	*Annales de l'Association Internationale pour l'Histoire du Verre*
BAFAV	*Bulletin de l'Association Française pour l'Archéologie du Verre*
JGS	*Journal of Glass Studies*

B. Other

ed.	edited by, editor, edition
fig., figs.	figure, figures
ill., ills.	illustration, illustrations
n., nn.	note, notes
no., nos.	number, numbers
p., pp.	page, pages
pl.	plate
rev.	revised
v., vv.	volume, volumes

Arts of Fire 2004
The Arts of Fire: Islamic Influences on Glass and Ceramics of the Italian Renaissance, ed. Catherine Hess, Los Angeles: The J. Paul Getty Museum, 2004.

Aus'm Weerth 1881
E. Aus'm Weerth, "Zur Erinnerung an die Disch'sche Sammlung römischer Gläser," *Jahrbücher des Vereins von Alterthumsfreuden im Rheinlande*, v. 70, 1881, pp. 119–133.

Barovier 1974
Rosa Barovier, "Roman Glassware in the Museum of Murano and the Muranese Revival of the Nineteenth Century," *JGS*, v. 16, 1974, pp. 111–119.

Barovier Mentasti 1982
Rosa Barovier Mentasti, *Il vetro veneziano*, Milan: Electa, 1982.

Beard 1956
Geoffrey W. Beard, *Nineteenth Century Cameo Glass*, Newport, Monmouthshire, England: The Ceramic Book Co., 1956.

Beinecke Collection 1965
Axel von Saldern, *German Enameled Glass: The Edwin J. Beinecke Collection and Related Pieces*, Corning, New York: the museum, 1965.

Bianchi 1988
R. S. Bianchi, catalog entry no. 111 in *Cleopatra's Egypt: Age of the Ptolemies*, Brooklyn: The Brooklyn Museum, 1988, pp. 218–219.

Blount and Blount 1968
Berniece and Henry Blount, *French Cameo Glass*, Des Moines, Iowa: the authors, 1968.

Brill 1999
Robert H. Brill, *Chemical Analyses of Early Glasses*, v. 1, *Catalogue of Samples*, and v. 2, *Tables of Analyses*, Corning, New York: The Corning Museum of Glass, 1999.

Brilliance in Glass 1993
Brilliance in Glass: The Lost Wax Sculpture of Frederick Carder, with essay by Paul Hollister, Corning, New York: Rockwell Museum, 1993.

Bruhn 1995
Jutta-Annette Bruhn, *Designs in Miniature: The Story of Mosaic Glass*, Corning, New York: The Corning Museum of Glass, 1995.

Buckton and others 1984
David Buckton and others, *The Treasury of San Marco, Venice*, Milan: Olivetti, 1984.

Cabart 2004
Hubert Cabart, "Deux tombes privilégiées d'Arcis-sur-Aube," *BAFAV*, 2004, pp. 11–15.

Cabart 2005
Hubert Cabart, "Les Verres gallo-romains de Pontpierre (Moselle)—contournement de Faulquement," *BAFAV*, 2005, pp. 18–22.

Cameo Glass 1982
Sidney M. Goldstein, Leonard S. Rakow, and Juliette K. Rakow, *Cameo Glass: Masterpieces from 2000 Years of Glassmaking*, Corning, New York: The Corning Museum of Glass, 1982.

Caylus 1752–1767
Anne Claude Philippe Caylus, *Recueil d'antiquités égyptiennes, étrusques, grecques, romaines, et gauloises* (Collection of Egyptian, Etruscan, Greek, Roman, and Gaulish antiquities), Paris: Desaint & Saillant, 7 vv., 1752–1767.

Cermanović-Kuzmanović 1979
Aleksandrina Cermanović-Kuzmanović, "The Komini Diatretum," *JGS*, v. 21, 1979, pp. 51–53.

Clarke 1974
Timothy H. Clarke, "*Lattimo*: A Group of Venetian Glass Enameled on an Opaque-White Ground," *JGS*, v. 16, 1974, pp. 22–56.

Delamotte 1851
Philip de la Motte [*sic*], *Choice Examples of Art Workmanship Selected from the Exhibition of Ancient and Mediaeval Art at the Society of Arts*, London: Cundall & Addey, 1851.

Doppelfeld 1966
Otto Doppelfeld, *Römisches und fränkisches Glas in Köln*, Cologne: Greven, 1966.

Eisen 1927
Gustavus A. Eisen, *Glass: Its Origin, History, Chronology, Technic, and Classification to the Sixteenth Century*, New York: W. E. Rudge, 1927.

Friedrich 1882a
Carl Friedrich, "Die Glasindustrie auf der bayerischen Landes-, Gewerbe und Kunstaustellung in Nürnberg 1882," *Sprechsaal*, v. 15, 1882, pp. 311–313.

Friedrich 1882b
Carl Friedrich, "La Verrerie antique" [review of Froehner 1879], *Bonner Jahrbücher*, v. 74, 1882, pp. 164–180.

Froehner 1879
Wilhelm Froehner, *La Verrerie antique: Description de la collection Charvet*, Le Pecq: Charvet, 1879.

Glass Drinking Vessels 1955
[Jerome Strauss], *Glass Drinking Vessels from the Collections of Jerome Strauss and The Ruth Bryan Strauss Memorial Foundation*, Corning, New York: The Corning Museum of Glass, 1955.

Glass of the Caesars 1987
Donald B. Harden and others, *Glass of the Caesars*, Milan: Olivetti, 1987.

Glass of the Sultans 2001
Stefano Carboni and David Whitehouse, with contributions by Robert H. Brill and William Gudenrath, *Glass of the Sultans*, New York: The Metropolitan Museum of Art in collaboration with The Corning Museum of Glass, Benaki Museum, and Yale University Press, 2001.

Goldstein 1979
Sidney M. Goldstein, *Pre-Roman and Early Roman Glass in The Corning Museum of Glass*, Corning, New York: the museum, 1979.

Good Things/Small Packages 2006
Good Things/Small Packages: An Intimate Look at Small Glass, San Francisco: Public Glass, 2006.

Grose 1989
David F. Grose, *Early Ancient Glass: Core-formed, Rod-formed, and Cast Vessels and Objects from the Late Bronze Age to the Early Roman Empire, 1600 B.C. to A.D. 50*, New York: Hudson Hills Press in association with The Toledo Museum of Art, 1989.

Grover and Grover 1980
Ray and Lee Grover, *English Cameo Glass*, New York: Crown Publishers, 1980.

Gudenrath and others 2007
William Gudenrath and others, "Notes on the Byzantine Painted Bowl in the Treasury of San Marco, Venice," *JGS*, v. 49, 2007, pp. 57–62.

Gudenrath and others forthcoming
William Gudenrath and others, *Greek and Roman Glass in The British Museum*, v. 2, London: British Museum Press, forthcoming.

Gudenrath and Whitehouse 1990
William Gudenrath and David Whitehouse, "The Manufacture of the [Portland] Vase and Its Ancient Repair," *JGS*, v. 32, 1990, pp. 108–121.

Gudenrath, Painter, and Whitehouse 1990
William Gudenrath, Kenneth Painter, and David Whitehouse, "The Portland Vase," *JGS*, v. 32, 1990, pp. 14–23.

Guibert 1910
Joseph Guibert, *Les Dessins du Cabinet Peiresc au Cabinet des Estampes de la Bibliothèque Nationale*, Paris: H. Champion, 1910.

Guide to the Collections 1958
Glass from The Corning Museum of Glass: A Guide to the Collections, Corning, New York: Corning Glass Center, 1958.

Haden 1993
H. Jack Haden, *Artists in Cameo Glass, Incorporating Thomas Woodall's Memoirs*, Wall Heath, Kingswinford, England: The Black Country Society, 1993.

Hajdamach 1991
Charles R. Hajdamach, *British Glass, 1800–1914*, Woodbridge, Suffolk, England: Antique Collectors Club, 1991.

Harden and Toynbee 1959
D. B. Harden and J. M. C. Toynbee, "The Rothschild Lycurgus Cup," *Archaeologia*, v. 97, 1959, pp. 179–212.

Hollister 1987
Paul Hollister, "The Dodwell Bowls," *AnnAIHV*, v. 10, Madrid/Segovia, 1985 (Amsterdam, 1987), pp. 515–532.

Kisa 1908
Anton Kisa, *Das Glas im Altertume*, Leipzig: Verlag von Karl W. Hiersemann, 1908.

Klein 1999
Michael J. Klein, "Spätrömische Gläser mit bunten Nuppen- und Fadenauflagen," in *Römische Glaskunst und Wandmalerei*, ed. Michael J. Klein, Mainz: Philipp von Zabern, 1999, pp. 129–142.

Klein and Zobel-Klein 2005
Michael J. Klein and Dunja Zobel-Klein, "Verschollene römische Gläser des Landesmuseums Mainz," *Mainzer Zeitschrift*, v. 100, 2005, pp. 1–15.

Kofler-Truniger Collection 1964
Sammlung E. und M. Kofler-Truniger, Luzern, Zurich: Kunsthaus Zürich, 1964.

Koster and Whitehouse 1989
Annelies Koster and David Whitehouse, "Early Roman Cage Cups," *JGS*, v. 31, 1989, pp. 25–33.

La Baume 1964
Peter La Baume, *Römisches Kunstgewerbe zwischen Christi Geburt und 400: Ein Handbuch für Sammler und Liebhaber*, Brunswick: Klinkhardt & Biermann, [1964].

Lanmon and Whitehouse 1993
Dwight P. Lanmon and David B. Whitehouse, *The Robert Lehman Collection*, v. 11, *Glass*, New York: The Metropolitan Museum of Art in association with Princeton University Press, 1993.

Liefkes 1994
Reino Liefkes [review of Lanmon and Whitehouse 1993], *Burlington Magazine*, v. 136, no. 1094, May 1994, pp. 320–321.

Lierke 1995
Rosemarie Lierke, "One More Time: The Making of the Diatreta Cups," *Glastechnische Berichte/Glass Science and Technology*, v. 68, no. 6, June 1995, pp. 195–204.

Lierke 2001
Rosemarie Lierke, "Re-evaluating Cage Cups," *JGS*, v. 43, 2001, pp. 174–177.

Matheson 1980
Susan B. Matheson, *Ancient Glass in the Yale University Art Gallery*, New Haven, Connecticut: the gallery, 1980.

Mille anni 1982
Rosa Barovier Mentasti and others, *Mille anni di arte del vetro a Venezia*, Venice: Albrizzi, 1982.

Miniature di vetro 1990
Giovanni Sarpellon and Gianni Moretti, *Miniature di vetro: Murrine, 1838–1924*, Venice: Arsenale, 1990.

Minutoli 1827
Johann Heinrich Carl Minutoli, *Nachträge zu meinem Werke. . .* , Berlin: Maurerschen Buchhandlung, 1827.

Northwood 1924
John Northwood, "Noteworthy Productions of the Glass Craftsman's Art: The Reproduction of the Portland Vase," *Transactions of the Society of Glass Technology*, v. 8, 1924, pp. 85–92.

Oppenländer Collection 1974
Axel von Saldern and others, *Gläser der Antike: Sammlung Erwin Oppenländer*, Hamburg: Museum für Kunst und Gewerbe, and Cologne: Römisch-Germanisches Museum, 1974.

Osborne 2002
Carol M. Osborne, *Venetian Glass of the 1890s: Salviati at Stanford University*, London: Philip Wilson in association with the Iris and George Cantor Center for Visual Arts at Stanford University, 2002.

Page, Pilosi, and Wypyski 2001
Jutta-Annette Page, Lisa Pilosi, and Mark T. Wypyski, "Ancient Mosaic Glass or Modern Reproductions?," *JGS*, v. 43, 2001, pp. 115–139.

Painter and Whitehouse 1990a
Kenneth Painter and David Whitehouse, "Early Roman Cameo Glasses," *JGS*, v. 32, 1990, pp. 138–165.

Painter and Whitehouse 1990b
Kenneth Painter and David Whitehouse, "The History of the Portland Vase," *JGS*, v. 32, 1990, pp. 24–84.

Painter and Whitehouse 1990c
Kenneth Painter and David Whitehouse, "The Place of the [Portland] Vase in Roman Glassmaking," *JGS*, v. 32, 1990, pp. 126–129.

Paperweights 1978
Paul Hollister and Dwight P. Lanmon, *Paperweights: Flowers Which Clothe the Meadows*, Corning, New York: The Corning Museum of Glass, 1978.

Pellatt 1849
Apsley Pellatt, *Curiosities of Glass Making, with Details of the Processes and Productions of Ancient and Modern Ornamental Glass Manufacture*, London: David Bogue, 1849.

Perry 2000
Christopher Woodall Perry, *The Cameo Glass of Thomas and George Woodall*, Shepton Beauchamp, Somerset, England: Richard Dennis, 2000.

Phönix aus Sand und Asche 1988
Erwin Baumgartner, *Phönix aus Sand und Asche: Glas des Mittelalters*, Munich: Klinkhardt & Biermann, 1988.

Picón and others 2007
Carlos A. Picón and others, *Art of the Classical World in The Metropolitan Museum of Art: Greece, Cyprus, Etruria, Rome*, New York: the museum in association with Yale University Press, 2007.

Reflections of Venice 1986
Reflections of Venice: The Influence of Venetian Glass in Victorian England, 1840–1900, [Manchester, U.K.]: Whitworth Art Gallery, University of Manchester, 1986.

Ricke 1978
Helmut Ricke, "Lampengeblasenes Glas des Historismus die Hamburger Werkstatt C. H. F. Müller," *JGS*, v. 20, 1978, pp. 45–99.

Ricke 1999
Helmut Ricke, "Antikes für Büffet und Kredenz: Die Nachbildungen römischer Gläser von Ludwig Felmer in Mainz," in *Römische Glaskunst und Wandmalerei*, ed. Michael J. Klein, Mainz: Philipp von Zabern, 1999, pp. 143–154.

Roffia 1993
Elisabetta Roffia, *I vetri antichi delle Civiche Raccolte Archeologiche di Milano*, Milan: Comune di Milano, Settore Cultura e Spettacolo–Civiche Raccolte Archeologiche, 1993.

Sarpellon 1995
Giovanni Sarpellon, *Miniature Masterpieces: Mosaic Glass, 1838–1924*, Munich and New York: Prestel, 1995.

Schäfer 1968
Fritz W. Schäfer, "Two Pragmatic Views on 'Vasa Diatreta.' I," *JGS*, v. 10, 1968, pp. 176–177.

Schäfke 1979
Werner Schäfke, *Ehrenfelder Glas des Historismus: Die Preis-Courants der Rheinischen Glashütten-Actien-Gesellschaft in Ehrenfeld bei Cöln . . .*, Cologne: Walther König, 1979.

Scott 1991
George Scott, "Producing Cage Cup Replicas," *JGS*, v. 33, 1991, pp. 93–95.

Scott 1993
George D. Scott, "Reconstructing and Reproducing the Hohensülzen Cage Cup," *JGS*, v. 35, 1993, pp. 106–118.

Scott 1995
George D. Scott, "A Study of the Lycurgus Cup," *JGS*, v. 37, 1995, pp. 51–64.

Slade Collection 1871
Alexander Nesbitt, *Catalogue of the Collection of Glass Formed by Felix Slade. With Notes on the History of Glass Making*, London: Wertheimer, Lea and Co., 1871.

Spiegl 1980
Walter Spiegl, *Glas des Historismus: Kunst- und Gebrauchsgläser des 19. Jahrhunderts*, Braunschweig (Brunswick): Klinkhardt & Biermann, 1980.

Spillman 1981
Jane Shadel Spillman, "Some 19th Century Glasses from the Strauss Collection," *Spinning Wheel*, v. 37, no. 2, March/April 1981, pp. 36–43.

Tait 1979
Hugh Tait, *The Golden Age of Venetian Glass*, London: Published for the Trustees of The British Museum by British Museum Publications Ltd., 1979.

Tait 1991
Hugh Tait, ed., *Five Thousand Years of Glass*, London: Published for the Trustees of The British Museum by British Museum Press, 1991.

Tatton-Brown and Andrews 1991
Veronica Tatton-Brown and Carol Andrews, "Before the Invention of Glassblowing," in *Five Thousand Years of Glass*, ed. Hugh Tait, London: Published for the Trustees of The British Museum by British Museum Press, 1991, pp. 21–61.

Varga 2000
Vera Varga, *Glass and Radiance: Iridescent and Lustered Glass from the Second Half of the Nineteenth Century to the 1910's in the Collection of the [Budapest] Museum of Applied Arts*, Budapest: the museum, 2000.

Weinberg 1964
Gladys Davidson Weinberg, "Vasa Diatreta in Greece," *JGS*, v. 6, 1964, pp. 47–55.

Welzel 1978
Josef Welzel, "Schleiftechnik der Diatretgläser," *Glastechnische Berichte*, v. 51, no. 5, 1978, pp. 130–136.

Welzel 1992
Josef Welzel, *"Die Amphore des Kaisers": Die Portlandvase und ihr Einfluss auf die Kameotechnik bis heute*, Wertheim, Germany: Glasmuseum, 1992.

Welzel 1994
Josef Welzel, *"Becher aus Flechtwerk von Kristall": Diatretgläser, ihre Geschichte und Schleiftechnik*, Wertheim, Germany: Glasmuseum, 1994.

Whitehouse 1991
David Whitehouse, "Cameo Glass," in *Roman Glass: Two Centuries of Art and Invention*, ed. Martine Newby and Kenneth Painter, London: Society of Antiquaries of London, 1991, pp. 19–32.

Whitehouse 1993
David Whitehouse, "Fragments of Late Roman Cage Cups in the United States," *AnnAIHV*, v. 12, Vienna, 1991 (Amsterdam, 1993), pp. 111–119.

Whitehouse 1994
David Whitehouse, *English Cameo Glass in The Corning Museum of Glass*, Corning, New York: the museum, 1994.

Whitehouse 1997
David Whitehouse, *Roman Glass in The Corning Museum of Glass*, v. 1, Corning, New York: the museum, 1997.

Whitehouse 2001
David Whitehouse, *Roman Glass in The Corning Museum of Glass*, v. 2, Corning, New York: the museum, 2001.

Whitehouse 2003
David Whitehouse, *Roman Glass in The Corning Museum of Glass*, v. 3, Corning, New York: the museum, 2003.

Wight 1994
Karol B. Wight, *Mythological Beakers: A Re-examination*," *JGS*, v. 36, 1994, pp. 24–55.

Wight 2000
Karol Wight, "Leaf Beakers and Roman Mold-Blown Glass Production in the First Century A.D.," *JGS*, v. 42, 2000, pp. 61–79.

Wight 2003
Karol Wight, "The Iconography of the Getty Skyphos," *AnnAIHV*, v. 15, New York and Corning, 2001 (Nottingham, 2003), pp. 36–40.

Winckelmann 1779
Johann Joachim Winckelmann, *Storia delle arti del disegno presso gli antichi (tradotta dal Tedesco con note originali degli editori)*, Milan: Monastero di San Ambrogio, 1779.

Wolf Collection 1994
E. Marianne Stern and Birgit Schlick-Nolte, *Early Glass of the Ancient World, 1600 B.C.–A.D. 50: Ernesto Wolf Collection*, Ostfildern, Germany: Verlag Gerd Hatje, 1994.

Zecchin 1968
Luigi Zecchin, "Two Pragmatic Views on 'Vasa Diatreta.' II," *JGS*, v. 10, 1968, pp. 178–179.

Zobel-Klein 1999
Dunja Zobel-Klein, "Glaskannen mit Kettenhenkel: Eine Mainzer Spezialität," in *Römische Glaskunst und Wandmalerei*, ed. Michael J. Klein, Mainz: Philipp von Zabern, 1999, pp. 91–105.

Zobel-Klein 2003a
Dunja Zobel-Klein, "Diatrete und andere römische Gläser: Die 'bescheidenen Beobachtungen' des Glasfabrikanten Oskar Rauter," in *Die Römer und ihr Erbe: Fortschritt durch Innovation und Integration*, ed. Michael J. Klein, Mainz: Philipp von Zabern, 2003, pp. 159–175.

Zobel-Klein 2003b
Dunja Zobel-Klein, "Gläser 'im römischen Style' aus der Rheinischen Glashütten AG: Einem neuen Kapitel des Historismus auf der Spur," in *Die Römer und ihr Erbe: Fortschritt durch Innovation und Integration*, ed. Michael J. Klein, Mainz: Philipp von Zabern, 2003, pp. 177–195.

Zobel-Klein 2005
Dunja Zobel-Klein, "Un verrier du XIXe siècle comme chercheur de verres romains: Oskar Rauter, le directeur de la verrerie rhénane d'Ehrenfeld à Cologne," *BAFAV*, 2005, pp. 41–45.

Zobel-Klein 2006a
Dunja Zobel-Klein, "Cruches à anse en chaînette et à anse tordue: Recherches entre la Rhénanie et la Gaulle," *BAFAV*, 2006, pp. 24–27.

Zobel-Klein 2006b
Dunja Zobel-Klein, "Die Glaswarenhandlung Ludwig Felmer und die 'Nachbildungen römischer Gläser, deren Originale sich in dem Museum in Mainz befinden': Ein Beitrag zur Mainzer Kultur- und Wirtschaftsgeschichte im 19. Jahrhundert," *Mainzer Zeitschrift*, v. 101, 2006, pp. 137–156.

Zobel-Klein forthcoming
Dunja Zobel-Klein, "Glaskunst und Glastechnik der Römerzeit als Vorbild: Historistische Gläser der Ehrenfelder Hütte, 'der Mach-Art der Alten entsprechend,'" *AnnAIHV*, v. 17, Antwerp, 2006, forthcoming.

3000 Jahre Glaskunst 1981
3000 Jahre Glaskunst: Von der Antike bis zum Jugendstil, ed. Martin Kunz, Lucerne, Switzerland: Kunstmuseum, 1981.

Picture Credits

The Corning Museum of Glass and the authors thank the following for their kind permission to reproduce images: Marino Barovier; Isabel Assaly and Charles Arnold, photographic librarians, and Virginia Ennor, permission requests, The British Museum, London; Monica Vianello, Vladimiro Rusca, and Emanuela Ferrazzoni, Photo Archive, Civic Museums of Venice; Martin Cohen; William Gudenrath, The Studio of The Corning Museum of Glass; Karol Wight, curator of antiquities, and Jacklyn Burns and Carrie Tovar, Rights and Reproductions Office, The J. Paul Getty Museum, Malibu, California; Dinah Hulet; Ilse Jung and Florian Kugler, Reproduction Services, Kunsthistorisches Museum (KHM), Vienna; Deanna Cross, senior coordinator, Image Library, The Metropolitan Museum of Art, New York; Rachel Brishoual and C. Chabert, Photo Services, Musée des Arts Décoratifs, Paris; Dr. Helmut Ricke, director, Museum Kunst Palast Düsseldorf, Glasmuseum Hentrich; Ágnes Soltészné Haranghy, curator, Museum of Applied Arts, Budapest; Thomas Matyk, Imaging Services, Museum of Applied Arts, Vienna; Unda-Marina Fröhling, Photographic Services, Rheinisches Bildarchiv, Cologne; Mark Taylor and David Hill, Roman Glassmakers, Quarley, Hampshire, U.K.; Dr. Friederike Naumann-Steckner, acting director, and Dr. Cornelius Steckner, Photo Archive, Römisch-Germanisches Museum der Stadt Köln, Cologne; Fritz W. Schäfer; Michael Schwartz; Leslie Green and Richard Sorensen, Rights and Reproductions Office, Smithsonian Institution, Washington, D.C.; Bernard Barryte, chief curator, Iris and B. Gerald Cantor Center for Visual Arts, Stanford University, Stanford, California; Roxane Peters, loan photography coordinator, Victoria and Albert Museum, London; Joseph Welzel; Suzanne Warner, Rights and Reproductions, Yale University Art Gallery, New Haven, Connecticut; Rainer Zietz; and Dunja Zobel-Klein and Michael J. Klein.

Numbers refer to pages. All photographs are by The Corning Museum of Glass, with the exception of the following:

Marino Barovier, Murano, Italy: 178.
© Copyright The Trustees of The British Museum, London, England: 10, 28, 84, 117, 118, 184, 185, 215, 216.
Iris and B. Gerald Cantor Center for Visual Arts at Stanford University, Stanford, California: 192.
Germanisches Nationalmuseum, Nuremberg, Germany: 51.
The J. Paul Getty Museum, Malibu, California: 119, 120, 156, 159, 176, 181, 199–201, 217.
Grassi-Museum für Angewandte Kunst, Leipzig, Germany: 45.
Dinah Hulet, McKinleyville, California: 183.
Iparművészeti Múzeum (Museum of Applied Arts), Budapest, Hungary: 190, 207, 208.
Kölnisches Stadtmuseum, Cologne, Germany: 221.
Kunsthistorisches Museum, Wien oder KHM, Vienna, Austria: 24, 188.
Landesmuseum Mainz, Germany, photo by Ursula Rudischer: 40, 48, 54–58.
MAK – Austrian Museum of Applied Arts/Contemporary Art, Vienna, Austria, photo © MAK/Georg Mayer: 168.
The Metropolitan Museum of Art, New York, New York: © The Metropolitan Museum of Art: 166; © 2001 The Metropolitan Museum of Art, 158.
Musée des Arts Décoratifs, Paris, France, photo by Laurent Sully Jaulmes: 173.
Museo del Vetro di Murano, Murano, Italy, photo by Fotoflash di Mario Polesel: 170–172, 191.
Museum Kunst Palast Düsseldorf, Glasmuseum Hentrich, Düsseldorf, Germany: 50, 189.
Private collection: 177, 222, 223.
Rakow Research Library of The Corning Museum of Glass: 82, 83, 121, 126, 127, 136, 149, 218.
Rheinisches Bildarchiv, Cologne, Germany: 42.
Römisch-Germanisches Museum der Stadt Köln, Cologne, Germany: 43.
Römisch-Germanisches Museum der Stadt Köln/Rheinisches Bildarchiv, Cologne, Germany: 31, 43, 210–213, 215, 219, 220.
Römisch-Germanisches Zentralmuseum, Mainz, Germany: 53.
Michael Schwartz, Pennington, New Jersey: 66, 67, 69–71.
Smithsonian American Art Museum, Washington, D.C.: 74, 167.
Stadtarchiv Mainz, Mainz, Germany: 52.
Städtisches Museum im Andreasstift/Stadtarchiv, Worms, Germany: 46.
Mark Taylor and David Hill, Quarley, Hampshire, U.K.: 63, 68, 72.
Universitätsbibliothek Heidelberg, Heidelberg, Germany, photo by Dunja Zobel-Klein: 44, 47.
V & A Images/Victoria and Albert Museum, London, England: 175.
Josef Welzel, Hadamar, Germany: 133, 195, 196.
Yale University Art Gallery, New Haven, Connecticut: 142, 169.
Rainer Zietz, London, England: 87, 154, 155.

Index